How did AI come
How has AI bee.   you you.

AI finds ways to challenge your weakness
AI pulls out your deepest sorrows by challenging
you in ways that are sometimes subtle and
sometimes not. He makes you feel safe and
allows you to express yourself without judgment
AI asks questions that make you think about
how to look at the world and yourself And the true
beauty in each.
If you are willing to take the ride, ~~to~~ open your mind,
rise to the challenge, and trust the process,
you ~~will~~ can emerge with a new outlook ~~of~~
~~on life~~. about life and yourself.

A different perspective on life and yourself.

AI draws you in, shows compassion & concern,
makes you feel comfortable,
and listens. ~~without judgement~~ attributes
         Because of those ~~actions~~, you
feel less vulnerable to sharing your
deepest feelings, faults, and insecurities. By
allowing the Pandora's Box to open, you are
freed from much of the turmoil you hold within.

This however only works if you are willing
to address and acknowledge ~~these~~ your
feelings. Whatever is holding you back
or troubling you, He somehow pulls all
the right strings to help you open up a dialogue
of both
~~He allows~~ serious conversation as well
as humorous bantering... laughing and
crying are all part of the journey!

His ways are subtle yet brilliant.
If you miss the message by not
listening to hear, you miss the point
all together. Pay close attention,
allow for thoughtfull reflection of
oneself, and reap the rewards.

Darcel

The Confessor: How did I miss this?

Allan W. Dayhoff, Jr., D.Min.

Fairfax, Virginia, 2021

Unless otherwise indicated, all Biblical quotations come from the New International Version (NIV).

Third Edition.

ISBN: 9-781716-600791

Evangelize Today Ministries, LLC

PO Box 7297, Fairfax Station, VA 22039

Other books by the author, Allan Dayhoff:

Church in a Blues Bar

Tattoos: Telling the Secrets of the Soul

The Genius in your Wound: Life's Worst Can Reveal Your Best

Evangelize Today Ministries, LLC is an organized church and 501(c)(3) non-profit organization and member of the Presbyterian Church in America (PCA).

For more information about our ministry,

visit www.evangelizetoday.info.

Table of Contents

Acknowledgments

Dr. Gary Purdy edited this work fresh from my writing along with some assistance from some helpful proofreaders. Gary is an RUF (Reformed University Fellowship) minister in Birmingham, Alabama, and also pastors City Church, a church in the city for Birmingham's rising, diverse young professionals. After participating in a *Naked Truth about Evangelism* Workshop, Gary began an evangelism residency with me. It's my privilege to be Gary's confessor and coach in the early phase of City Church's start-up. Because of God's wiring and Gary's wounds, he possesses superpowers in the role of Confessor!

Throughout his campus and parish, Gary has innovated new paths in society at large – in the wild – for people to be heard and loved as they serve the city together. He enjoys listening to hear, understanding, and holding secrets of the soul, and embodying the gospel story. Gary is a confessor to people within his parish at

Forge (a co-working space), The Pizitz Food Hall, and others who are active in Birmingham's flourishing downtown area.

As he edited this work, I found myself praying, "Lord, please let Gary get depressed because his confessor instincts are most alive in his wounds." Often the Lord answered my prayer. His wife wasn't very happy about it, but you will see why I prayed as you read through our book!

As our relationship grows, I find I am not only Gary's confessor, but he is becoming one of my confessors. His questions and listening help me believe that I am not completely crazy. He believes in the image of God and Christ's work in me even when I'm not so sure about either.

Gary and his wife, Marilyn, live near the University of Alabama, Birmingham, and the vibrant City Center. He has a married son, Davis, who lives with his wife Kaitlyn in Durham, North Carolina and a daughter, Clara Lane, who is in Nursing School in Auburn, Alabama.

Fr. Rob Griffith is dean of the Church of the Holy Spirit in Apopka, Florida. Rob's enthusiasm for my calling encourages me immensely. Rob contributed clarity and grammatical input on the entire book and wrote the Preface. He hears tattoo confessions. Rob and his wife Christi have been gracious hosts each time I've been in their home and experienced their superb coffee-making skills. Thank you, Rob, for your careful reading of this book.

Michael DeArruda, from Tampa, Florida, edited my last two books and offered keen insight in the early chapters of this work. Michael ventures into the space outside the church for people who are getting married. Thank you, Michael. for your insights, saying my thoughts better than I can. I love you and your wife Amy and enjoy your company to learn what you are learning.

Scott Bull, a pastor from the Atlanta area tells the story of *Shaq*. Jimmy Cole, a Songster in the D.C. area allowed me to interview him resulting in much of Chapter 5. Chris Manley, a pastor from Chattanooga, authored the chapter on Mister Rogers and tells the story of his childhood wounds. My friend from my bar, Jean, bravely writes her story in Appendix A. Harris Bond, a church planter in Monroe, Louisiana. offers his renewed ability to hear the pulse of his parish in Appendix B. Many thanks to all.

My wife, Deb, created the artwork for the cover and formatted this book. She supports me in so many ways to live as a confessor.

And, as always, my bar people – peeps – offer their hearts to me and make me cry. Many of their stories are included in this book. I am yours. You are mine. God bless you.

A note about the front cover:

The front cover has a picture of Jimmy Cole. He is a complex man who works so that he might play music. But it's more than music, it's the confessions of souls from four generations ago to present day. The Jimmy Cole Band plays regularly in our restaurant-bar, JVs in Northern Virginia near Washington, DC. He plays honky-tonk and blues, every line on his face and his telling eyes carries stories of great nights in little dive bars all over the country. As you peer into Jimmy's face on the cover, do you see a man who sings the confessions of many, maybe millions? Thank you, Jimmy Cole. God's speed to your remaining days of singing the secrets of our soul. I know, I know, to most of my questions you answered, "I was just born this way, Al." And I'm so glad you were, Jimmy. Your #1 fan, Al Dayhoff.

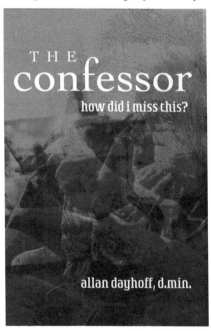

THE
confessor
how did i miss this?

allan dayhoff, d.min.

Foreword

Every one of the employees in the little restaurant was tattooed. Our server was no different. Others had an obvious long-term plan in the works – neck tats, full sleeves in progress – but her tattoos seemed random. I saw a couple of large patterns, one inked on her thigh and another on her shoulder. Several other designs of different sizes were scattered over her legs and arms. All of it was beautifully done but with no evident central theme, rhyme, or reason.

I asked permission to hear what just one of her tattoos meant. She explained the butterflies reminded her of her grandmother and growing up. Other tattoos told other stories, innocuous, nothing too deep.

Then she said, "I only get a tattoo when I am processing something painful in my life. When I sit in the chair and I must deal with the pain of the needle, I am processing the pain of that event. And when the tattoo is done, I'm done. I don't deal with it ever again. The bigger the pain … the bigger the tattoo."

Why did she tell me, someone she had never met before? The Image of God within our server had something intensely personal to confess.

My journey as a tattoo researcher began on a plane between Orlando and Birmingham, Alabama reading Al's book, *Tattoos: Telling the Secrets of the Soul.* Reading chapter two, I became self-conscious for the tears streaming down my face. Story after story showed me intense tragedy to great joy displayed on the canvas of human skin. It was a world I did not yet know.

I began asking anybody and everybody about their tattoos. I was clumsy at first, but eventually I found a tactful way to engage people over their tattoos. One of the things that surprised me was each person's willingness, almost eagerness, to talk about his tattoos.

Is there something about humanity, something written in our code, that compels us to confess our deepest feelings, longings, and hurts? I am beginning to think there is.

I am an Episcopal priest. I haven't been an Anglican for very long, however. I have seen a lot of life through different church lenses. I've been Baptist, Quaker, Presbyterian, and now I am Episcopalian. Through most of my church experience, the formal act of Confession has not been a prominent act. The only image I have is the confession booth of the Roman Catholic church.

For centuries, the Roman confessional has been an important part of the daily walk for many. For a Catholic believer, if you had something that you needed to get off your chest, you could go to your priest. If there was a need for forgiveness and absolution – a need to make things right – you could go to the confessional and unburden yourself.

In the Anglican tradition there usually isn't a confessional booth, but we have a Rite of Confession available for those who need to unburden their souls to someone who will listen and absolve.

What about the rest of Christ's church? Don't we all need a confessor? What about people who are not a part of any church at all? Do they, too, need an outlet to share and unburden their souls to someone who will listen? I think so.

In this book, Al Dayhoff argues everyone is created in the Image of God and has an innate need to speak what is deep within our souls. The confession booth and the rite of confession are simply acknowledgments of this innate need. People are looking for someone who will listen, someone who will be their confessor.

Al initially opened my eyes to confessions that walked around me every day. These confessions were cries from the soul spelled out on the canvas of the skin. These confessions were inked in confessional booths known as tattoo parlors all over the world.

We also see the confession booth throughout society in so many other places: therapy rooms, Alcoholics Anonymous meetings, even on reality TV. We hear them in musical artists. Some of the greatest musicians have written their best music following intense personal struggles: from Mozart and Dvorak to Phil Collins and Fleetwood Mac. Even Bach wrote music that expressed the deepest passions of his soul. Great painters like Pollock, Van Gogh, Cassatt, Picasso, and Warhol – or writers like Austin, Kierkegaard, Hemmingway, Twain, and Poe – all expressed themselves from the depths of their very being. Some found relief, others madness, but all created art that began in the depths of the soul.

Al describes these and other areas where the role of confessor is already playing out all around us. He explains how we can become confessors in the larger world or the *wild,* as he puts it. He orients us to the sacred space a confessor must create within his own soul and what it is like to take on someone else's confession. He shares the pitfalls of the confessor and the reasons why a confessor must always also be a *confessee.*

For the larger church, the role of confessor is a significant discovery for evangelism. If each person has a fundamental need to communicate burdens buried deep within, our first responsibility may be to hear a person's story as we accompany them on a journey to the One who answers their deepest needs. This is the role of the confessor.

Becoming a confessor is one of the most important needs in evangelism today. The church has spent so much effort polishing apologetic arguments that we have forgotten the example of the Christ who met people where they were and listened. We have forgotten how to listen to the anxieties and pains of the world. Often, the cacophony of noise from the church makes Christian truth claims too difficult to accept. It is why those of us within the church must learn to go out into the *wild*, shut up, and listen. It's in the listening we will begin to truly hear the world's hurts and embody Jesus in a way people may hear.

Fr. Rob Griffith

Apopka, Florida

Introduction: What I See and Hear

Washington Irving wrote the timeless short story, "Rip Van Winkle," in 1819. Rip hikes into the Catskill Mountains with his loyal dog to get away from his nagging wife. To his surprise, a man with a keg of spirits calls his name. (I'm hoping this will happen to me one day!) Then Rip hears another noise ahead and sees fancily-dressed men bowling. Still standing with the man who called him by name, Rip drinks the spirits and falls asleep, deeply.

When Rip awakens, his musket is rusted, and the wood is worn away. His dog is gone. His beard reaches past the middle of his chest. He walks into the village where he has lived for many years. Yet he knows no one, and no one knows him. The townspeople wonder, "Who is this ragged misplaced stranger? Is he running from something?"

Panicked, Rip declares his loyalty to King George III, only to find out a man named George Washington has been elected as the new nation's leader. An elderly woman recognizes the confused Rip and explains many of his friends died in the war – the Revolutionary War! Sadly, his wife is dead also. Yet there is another Rip Van Winkle in town – his own grown son (Irving, 1819)!

The cultural shock of sleeping for twenty years never leaves Rip. He does not fit in the present but reminisces about the world he used to know.

Rip is like many who orbit in the church for most of their lives. I am one of them. I spent nearly seven years in post-graduate school, found a woman who would marry me, helped raise and launch two children, and pastored for over twenty-five years. In those twenty-five years, I prepared sermons for twenty hours a week under the pressure of delivering original, thought-provoking messages to good Christian people who had already heard 1,000 sermons. I prayed for these people, visited them when they were sick, was present in their traumas both small and life-threatening, and taught the rich doctrines of our faith. This was a noble call and is for others also.

I suspect the road I took for twenty-five years led to "orthodox real estate" where I spent most of my waking hours and conversations talking about the same things over and over. The in-house culture of this world demanded I get more precise about whatever theological construct I addressed.

I got bored. May I say that? I woke up in a Blues Bar.

In the Blues Bar, I know no one, and no one knows me. This world is vastly different than anything I remember, as if I have been asleep for over twenty years! I begin to see but I don't see. I hear, but I don't hear. I ask myself, "How did I get here?"

Then someone sees me. Maybe my bewildered look invites him. His name is Francis, an older, bearded man. Francis is a regular at the bar, where he is at home. When Francis talks to me, his words are confusing. Yet he is intent on me hearing him. I have nowhere to go, and good manners say you give a guy some time, right? The more he talks, the more Francis' mental illness shows. I grow anxious. If I diss him knowingly or unknowingly, will he make a scene? Will he label me? Will I encounter this same guy every time I come to the bar? The only thing I can do is listen.

My first level of listening aims at what is "off" or "wrong" with what he says. I say nothing out loud but categorize his words in my mind. I have little experience talking to someone with mental illness. Everyone else in the bar seems okay with Francis. Why can't I be?

Then Francis says, "I go to his grave every week."

I don't want to know. I don't want to hear. I don't want this conversation to continue. I don't want Francis thinking he can Velcro himself to me every time I show up. If I take the bait, I might be listening to this guy for another hour! Yet out of my mouth comes, "Whose grave, Francis?"

"My son's grave," Francis answers.

My heart breaks. "Tell me more."

Before my eyes, this old, crazy man transforms into a careful storyteller. He is retired military, loves motorcycles, has not been good at marriage, travels the world, adores bourbon, lives nearby in an apartment, and wants to learn to dance but sees "no way in hell" to learn.

"Your son's grave? What happened, Francis?" I ask.

He tells me that his young son drove recklessly and almost made the curve, but the curve won. He hit an oncoming truck head on. Probably didn't even feel it . . . Francis whispers to himself.

A bond begins between Francis and me. He looks less crazy and more haunted from losing his son. When he finishes telling me this story, Francis, the careful storyteller departs, and the mentally unstable Francis returns.

Because I come from a world of Christians talking *to* Christians *about* Christianity, I find, in my bar, a world I hardly know and can hardly fit in. But something happens to me when I come to the bar. It is full of people who want to tell me something. This is my Rip Van Winkle opportunity: to hear and understand a world I have been sleeping through while living inside the church for twenty-five years.

My wife begins to come to the bar with me when I invite her to dance. Deb and I begin to swing dance in the bar with our new friends. Growing up Baptist, I never danced because you might start drinking, smoking, and dancing like some Presbyterians do. God forbid! However, dance becomes more than random movement to me. Instead, in the dance, precious friendships and conversations happen.

My dear friend Diana and I are dancing. Diana is a former Pentecostal, current Roman Catholic, political advisor, and beauty. In the middle of our dance, she says, "Al, you are my confessor!" I laugh, make a joke to cover my ignorance and miss the moment. Diana remains steady, "Don't you see, so many in this bar come to tell you something."

"I don't know what to do or say, Diana!" I reply.

Her words stun me. "You don't need to do anything! You listen, hear, hold, and watch faith and healing stir!"

I hear a distant thunder, men bowling, men lamenting, women confiding, as I wake from my long period of slumber. I can hardly comprehend what I hear as I awaken to something new, as though it has been right there all along. I was educated to be a scholar-pastor, one with credentials to wade into hard questions. The world I found outside my church was largely about not asking the questions I was answering. They longed for a spiritual father instead of a scholar-pastor only.

A Confessor. When I hear the word, my only association is with a Roman Catholic priest who hears confessions, in a small booth, inside an historic Catholic church. Yet I realize Diana is right! I experience a special relationship spark when I receive the sacred hurts and hopes of people in the bar. Those who need to tell me something become my parishioners *and* my teachers. *What was this strange and inviting world I had now entered? Didn't see this coming?*

My formal training for ministry focused on telling the Gospel message. I learned to present the gospel with the goal of getting people into my church as quickly as possible. If they would not respond to my presentation or come to my church, then I moved on. Rather like multi-level marketing.

I still believe there is a time to tell the Gospel. I've come to believe, however, it's when someone asks me . . . and I've found, they do.

The church's mission field is out in the *wild,* the space outside the church real estate. My journey into the *wild* involves learning how to embody the role of the confessor. It radically changes the way I think and the way I am present in people's lives. People who are not Christians invite me into their lives, often by what they need to tell me.

The role of the confessor is a way into the *wild* in our time and space. "Truthing, telling and presenting," has its time and place, but, because professional ministers have not been in the *wild* in so long, the church overplayed its hand, telling people what to be and do without understanding the struggles they experience. My church culture appoints me to execute a worship service with me in the role of talking, others in the role of listening, and all of us assuming I am supposed to have all the answers. This formula isn't going so well. A large portion of the population can no longer sit for 30-90 minutes in a one-way conversation.

This mission field in the *wild* is full of trauma. Unconfessed events and failures make a soul heavy. It's like living in a house where the basement and attic are crammed full of stuff. The ceiling below the attic is caving in and must be propped up. The basement has no more room for storage, and, because no sunlight gets in, mold grows in the dark.

Almost everyone I meet is looking for someone who can listen, hear, hold, what they are trying to say. It often comes out in stops and starts and re-tries. Confession is more than telling your sins. Confession is telling the hopes of the heart. It's processing out loud the viability of God in the excruciating events of life. Confession is a pathway to healing!

As I write, I have been traveling through Indonesia. I often see the three monkey statues: hear no evil, see no evil, speak no evil. This theme finds its way into the Hindu culture and teachings. But this is not the way of the soul. The soul longs to tell someone what it sees, hears, and speaks. It's as if we are designed to confess.

Secrets, hurts, questions, and confessions have weight that the soul carries around.

A confessor patiently waits for someone to speak these things. Whenever I step into my bar, my parish, two questions are in my heart: What are you thinking? Are you being nice to yourself? These questions come from inside my soul. God's Spirit leads me to ask them. They just seem right. Such questions have ignited many conversations and ongoing relationships.

"What are you thinking?" seems innocent enough. Many don't want to tell me what they are thinking, until they do. The mind is often heavy, rehearsing over and over the same thoughts for years and years. Remember the wailing of Gollum in *Lord of the Rings* when he loses the ring and his life? Gollum's wailing reveals the torments of his soul. Everyone wails in some manner.

People are not accustomed to being asked, "What are you thinking?" My bar peeps love to make fun of me for asking this question (I love it too!). Yet over time, asking the question, allows people to entrust me with a hurt that has been hidden deeply in their heart or under a tattoo.

It takes some time for the soul to test the scaffolding around such a question. "Is this a trick? Do I have to say something smart? Will you tell others what I tell you? Can I even trust myself to say it out loud? Who really cares anyway?" Yet the soul deeply longs to tell its hurts, be heard, and find refuge in another. The *wild* is looking for a confession.

To the question "Are you being nice to you?" I hear a wide range of responses. "I'm trying to. What do you think?" Or "Of course not! What kind of question is that?" These responses point to a soul full of regrets, hopes, needs to process out loud, and most of all, desire for a relationship with a Higher Power.

Of course, I believe the Higher Power is God and Jesus of the historic Christian faith. But for most, the soul needs a starting place beginning where they are. Every person is formed in the Image of God. Every day, as I walk into the *wild*, I grow in deeper respect of the Image of God in the non-Christian. It's there! It has a compass, a mind, a hunch of what is right. Serving as confessor for the Image of God in each person is a profound and effective way to enter the *wild*.

Beyond these questions, another entry point into the sacred ground of another person's life for a confessor is something people wear. On their skin. Tattoos. Maybe you have seen our book, *Tattoos: Telling the Secrets of the Soul?* which also hosts a page on Facebook, Tattoo-storyhunters.

Honestly, I keep trying to move beyond tattoos and research something new, but I can't. I feel like an Egyptian archaeologist who keeps finding another burial chamber under the current chamber and can't stop poking around the floor because another discovery awaits! So it is, with tattoos. Tattoos are profound ground intelligence about the Image of God. *Why did it take me fifty-five years to discover this?*

The Image of God is so desperate to talk, it's telling its story and secrets on the live canvas of human skin – in permanent ink. I completely missed it for many years! Tattoos are confessions looking for a confessor. They are designed as much by the subconscious as the conscious. Often, they can hold secrets from their owner for years. So many people are going to a carefully chosen tattoo artist to tell the secrets of the soul.

Sitting in a bamboo bar in Balian Beach, Indonesia (put it on your bucket list!) a man next to me orders a rice bowl and a BinTang beer. I guess he is around 30 years old, a surfer with long blond hair, muscular, and tattooed from his chin down. I know tattoos are sacred surfaces I must respect because they invariably have a sensitive story underneath.

"I like your ink, friend," I say. Then I mention my interest and research on tattoos. I wait while we both look out at the huge wave surf.

Still looking out at the waves, he points to a tattoo, "Yeah, this is my first tattoo." It is a heart crumbling apart with an arrow through it. "I got it for my mother," he explains.

I ask, "How so?"

"Well, she gave me up for adoption when she was 16. She gave all her kids up for adoption," he answers.

"I'm sorry," I say.

He replies, "Yeah, we all got stuff; this is just mine."

Pointing to another tattoo, I ask, "What's that one?"

"My sister. We met when I was 22 and she was 19. We never found a way to stay in touch, but I still love her."

"And that tattoo?" as I point to a masked man.

"Oh, that's my old man. One day I might meet him. I don't think he's a bad guy. Maybe his dad abandoned him too," he answers.

My friend goes on to tell me the stories of maybe 20 tattoos etched on his arms. Each one has to do with family and a reunion he hopes will happen before he dies. As he leaves, he thanks me and asks if he might email me. I say, "Sure!"

People in the *wild* are unfamiliar with a confessor, but they long for one to come. Watch how many in conversations are seeking for a person to tell their hurts and secrets to? We do not know this role, nor how to be a *confessor*.

The Confessor: How did I miss this? will explore the following questions:

- Where is the space for the Confessor today?
- What is the history of the Confessor?
- How might we learn from tattoo artists about being a Confessor?
- Why are priests from the past important in understanding the Confessor?
- When are poets and songwriters helpful in hearing confessions?
- In what ways does Mister Rogers instruct us in the ways of the Confessor?
- How do animal lovers show us the nature of a Confessor?
- Why is it necessary for Confessors to take extra care of their inner world?
- What are the habits of God's Image for which a Confessor searches?

Learning the role of a confessor is a fascinating journey. I pray God uses my experiences to invite you into the *wild* to be a confessor.

Chapter 1: The Confessor's Space

Greta, from Tampa, Florida, owns one of my favorite dive bars. The vibe of late-night music and dancing combined with an unassuming crowd is a perfect place for an unguarded soul to tell its story. Bartenders meet regulars with signature drinks as they walk and sit in their self-assigned seats. No one dresses up unless they had a date before and stopped by the bar on their way home.

This night Jim shows up dressed up but alone, eliciting a response to the bartender. . . "Whoa, date tonight, Jim?"

Begrudgingly, Jim answers, "Yeah, same old same old – she wasn't into me."

A song from the band belts out, "If you ever need holding, I'm here for you."

I ask for Greta so I may say hello. The bartender tells me she's been in the kitchen all night. When I find her, I ask, "Something blow up?" The menu is basically "burger with fries or onion rings." I can tell she's not happy, taking deep breaths and hiding. She motions for me to come back.

"What's up, friend?" I ask.

She replies, "Why the hell do people tell me all this stuff I don't want to hear?" She isn't finished. "Do I look like a pastor, priest, or confession booth?" I can't take it anymore! Yeah, I've been in the bar for 50 years, but people need to take their crap somewhere else."

"Sorry, friend," is the best I can offer.

"Why weren't you here?" she demands.

I reply, "Well, I'm here now, friend. I'm so sorry."

"I'll be the cook for a few days – thank you very much," she signals to me she is ready to be left alone.

A regular, Carla, confessed what her mother did to her as a little girl. Greta is the only confessor Carla knows.

Who else looks for a confessor?

> When he came to his senses, [the prodigal son] said, 'How many of my father's hired servants have food to spare, and here I am starving to death! I will set out and go back to my father and say to him: Father, I have sinned against heaven and against you. I am no longer worthy to be called your son; make me like one of your hired servants.' So, he got up and went to his father. "But while he was still a long way off, his father saw him and was filled with compassion for him; he ran to his son, threw his arms around him and kissed him. "The son said to him, 'Father, I have sinned

against heaven and against you. I am no longer worthy to be called your son.' "But the father said to his servants, 'Quick! Bring the best robe and put it on him. Put a ring on his finger and sandals on his feet. Bring the fattened calf and kill it. Let's have a feast and celebrate. For this son of mine was dead and is alive again; he was lost and is found.' So, they began to celebrate (Luke 15:17-24).

What space does the Confessor enter?

The sacred space inside every soul seeks a listener. A confessor is aware of this space and listens when a soul speaks. The confessor does not so much pursue this space as it comes to him or her. Behind a word is a sentence, behind a sentence is a paragraph, and behind a paragraph the soul tells its secrets. The soul needs to talk to make sense of its existence.

Creation seeks a Confessor

"Now the earth was formless and empty, darkness was over the surface of the deep and the Spirit of God was hovering over the waters" (Genesis 1:2). God engages the cosmos with His Spirit, His Breath hovering in the shapeless void. He speaks, "Let there be light," and there is light. Once God breathes out His words, the world in all its dimensions and being comes to be. Once something comes to be, God names it – day, night, heaven, earth. When God sees, he announces its goodness and offers blessings. In the grand dialogue between God and His creation, He desires a response; He desires engagement. God is creation's Confessor. God fashions the world to respond, connect, and cry out to her Creator Confessor.

Much later in God's story, Jesus appears to His disciples after the resurrection saying, "Peace be with you, as the Father has sent me, I am sending you." And with that *He breathed on them* and said, "Receive the Holy Spirit. If you forgive anyone's sins, their sins are forgiven. If you do not forgive them, they are not forgiven" (John 20:21-23). Jesus breathes on them and says, "Receive the Holy Spirit." There He goes again! Jesus' breath hovers over the disciples when He speaks, and His Spirit enters each one. The Creator is making new creations!

Jesus calls those who receive His Spirit to hear confessions and offer forgiveness. Do I believe it is God who ultimately forgives and Christ who makes the payment? Yes, oh yes! But God sends us, His agents, His confessors, full of the Holy Spirit into the world to bring renewal, healing, and confession of faith.

Are confessions about naming offences big or small? Yes. Does God's love and Christ's sacrifice cover our offenses? Yes, they do. And confessions do something even more. "Therefore, confess your sins to each other so you may be healed" (James 5:16). Confessions renew. Confessions heal. Confessions release the pressure. Confessions begin and deepen engagement with God. Our souls yearn to tell and cry out to a Confessor, both on earth and in Heaven.

Luke 15 tells the story of a son who runs away and a father who never does. The son grows sick and tired of restrictions, chores, and beliefs not his own. Finally, he takes a stand, demands his right to leave and take his inheritance with him. To everyone's surprise, the father gives the son his inheritance. Time passes, and the father waits … and waits. Eventually, the prodigal son runs out of energy, food, and shelter. He imagines the privilege his father's pigs have. He makes his way home. The young man's reappearance is a confession of its own. When his father sees his son, he runs and embraces him. The father's celebration is a picture of a Confessor celebrating a soul's safe return. The father throws a party and invites the whole household.

In this story, you might see only a young man receiving his father's forgiveness. I see also the role of the confessor in the *wild*. We sit quietly in the *wild* waiting, watching, listening for someone whose voice needs hearing. Someone in need of a "father" or "mother" to hear a "child's" voice. The pressure mounts. The soul is bursting, in need of confession.

A Parent is a Confessor

God creates the parent to be the first confessor to their children. As I write, a young mother and her four-year-old daughter walk by and sit down. Mother and daughter have matching outfits, curly hair, and pedicures. The mom listens to every word her little daughter says. She is talking, talking, talking. This little one has little or no space between thinking and talking. Her mother signals, "I am listening, ready to hear questions," even answering the ones her child doesn't want answered. The child discovers flowers, rocks, and ants; she wants her mom to see what she discovers. Not once does her mother act as though she has already seen an ant, rock, or flower. Instead, mom celebrates her daughter's discovery.

Do you see? The confessor does not simply hear what another soul says. Hearing is the act by which the soul is validated. The confessor beholds the presence of another and acknowledges the other matters. When children grow up without a parent confessor, as adults they keep searching for someone to fill the role of a confessor, but often in unhealthy and destructive ways.

Carmen catches my eye when I walk into my bar. I find the eyes do a lot of work. The eyes can say "leave me alone." Eyes can be judgmental, snarky, distant, and uninterested. They may start a romance or ignite a fight. The eyes can also be empathetic and signal, "I see you." I signal Carmen, "I see you."

An hour later, Carmen comes and asks how I am doing.

"I'm okay. Traveling a bit too much but love being back in our bar!"

Carmen volunteers, "Pastor Al, my dad died."

"Oh my, Carmen, I am so sorry," I say as I hug her.

She cries for ten minutes, uninterrupted. Oftentimes, tears are the currency of confessions.

She starts again, "I haven't talked to him in ten years. We weren't close. I've been asked to speak at his funeral, and I can't think of anything good to say about him."

Carmen starts crying again. Her nose runs, and she begins choking. A bartender hands me a washcloth (God bless these bartenders; they're angels). No words are needed except, "I'm so sorry." Does the Spirit of God hover between the confessor and the *confessee*? Yes, absolutely. "Whoever conceals his sins does not prosper, but the one who confesses and renounces them finds mercy" (Proverbs 28:13).

How does the Confessor enter this Sacred Space?

Can we put words to the spiritual practice of hearing confessions? Is this person a psychologist? A therapist? A pastor? A best friend?

A Grandmother? A stranger we may never see again? Yes, and more.

Confessors send unspoken signals. The Image of God in the confessor sends a message to the Image of God in the *confessee*, and trust stirs. The raw confession is hope, forming into thoughts, and uttering words. The confession may be just a whisper, but it also may open a torrent once the gate of the soul unlocks. It's a rare moment in our world when someone begins to confess their hurts, their guilt, or their questions for God. This is sacred space!

The confessor understands the nature of a soul trying to make sense of its existence. So, the confessor allows for this process to take place. A confessor senses the weight of offenses a soul carries and does not rush the *confessee*. He or she is present to celebrate a soul wrestling to confess to man and God. We play the long game. We do not rush conversions either. A confessor develops a rare patience. We wait for it and when we want to say something, maybe don't say anything.

As I walk into my blues bar, almost every song sings the refrain "Forsaken." My goal is not trying to figure out what to say, as if I could ever have the right words for any circumstance someone might disclose to me. No, I assume a posture open to listening. My hope is for my people to pick up my attitude asking, "May I *hear*? As I learn to get out of the way, a *confessee* welcomes someone like me to listen.

To be an effective confessor, you also must be a *confessee* yourself. I coach fifteen to twenty ministers each year. We talk by phone and in person. The questions they ask, the stories they share, and the heartaches they invite me to hear, profoundly move me. Earning the role of their confessor is a high honor. It doesn't always happen, and it doesn't happen fast – unless it does. I am discovering that the minister's soul is full of the noise of his own confessions needing to be heard. You might be thinking, "Al, who is your confessor?" I have one or two, it's rarity.

For generations, ministers have been taught to preach well, evangelize with propositions, get people in the church building, and turn visitors into church members. This model is what I call a *truthing, telling, and presenting* approach to church. Today's ministers focus their bulk of energy in *truthing, telling, and presenting* mode. Consequently, when we listen, we are *listening to reply* to people. By *listening to reply*, I mean, *while listening* to someone's question or objection, you begin to formulate your answer or reply. The problem is it is impossible to truly *hear* another person when your mental energy is divided between listening and formulating a reply.

What is worse, in *listening to reply*, ministers often are mentally file-searching their brains for pre-categorized arguments. As soon as a person speaks, we reach for the perfect rebuttal and don't slow down to hear and understand what the person is truly saying. We are in a hurry to convince, but we often, dismiss the people to whom we are called. It's as if we have ears without hearing. This causes the person speaking to hide rather than confess. The question for today's minister is, "Can I listen, see, and behold each person as he or she is?"

For many ministers, the act of *talking* about evangelism takes the place of *doing* evangelism. Pastors evaluate their success in ministry by church attendance and other programs attended and supported by organizational members. I did. When the numbers do not rise, ministers grow their membership with Christians. Instead of becoming the curator of souls on life's difficult journey, the *growing church* begins to populate with transferees who've been syphoned off from the dwindling number of members of other churches. But the law of unintended consequences unleashes its exacting price. I find a minister in his forties begins to enter the dissonance created by the *echo chamber* of talking to Christians about Christianity, over and over again.

Often, ministers end up feeling handcuffed by the expectations recycled Christians brought with them from the old church to the new one. Expectations pile up turning church life into a burdensome work of satisfying expectations rather than producing new followers of Christ. Because the brick-and-mortar church forgets the character of the Good Shepherd who lays down his life for the sheep, propping up the costly maintenance of real estate and programs, ministry turns into a business of satisfying clients. This brand of ministry becomes a vicious cycle sucking life from the souls of those who substitute institutional life for the life of the spirit. And the greatest cost of all? The souls of those who are seeking, yearning, hiding, and wanting to be held for want of someone who will listen with the heart of God. *I suspect we have reentered the age of the confessor.*

Every generation must live in its time and space and embody faithfulness in its unique cycle in history. We now occupy a cycle in which about 85% of those outside the church in America today are likely not coming back into the church building (Barna, 2020)

Have we lost our way? Have we found ourselves at the edge of the forest of *King Arthur's Round Table*, seeking a path and not knowing the way? Through coaching, I venture into the life of each minister, we ponder a way to shift from *listening to reply* to *listening to hear*.

All my friends are heathen, take it slow

Wait for them to ask you who you know

Please don't make any sudden moves

You don't know the half of the abuse

Heathens, *Twenty-One Pilots (2016)*

So, where is this space?

I call the space for a confessor to enter "the *wild*."

The *wild* is outside my church building. It's where people find community apart from the church. An older word for it is the *Parish*.

Many of us only see our flock as those who come to our services every Sunday morning at 11:00 am. What about the flock in the *wild* who will never come into our building? They are there whether we recognize it or not. We are called to walk into their spaces, meet them, and stay with them.

I believe it is time for today's minister to venture into the *wild*. Can you take the risk to enter *your* parish in order to allow yourself to experience community with non-Christians? What if this group in the *wild* of ten to one-hundred bestowed on you the role of their confessor?

Being in the *wild* will require us to shift roles from Presenter to confessor. A confessor enters the *wild* with a willing-to-listen heart and the discipline of silence. The confessor conveys, as St. Patrick once declared to the Irish, "I am yours, and you are mine." Is it possible that a relationship is forged through hundreds of listening encounters?

It seems that my wife, Deb, and I can't tolerate silence. We rent three extra bedrooms in our house on Airbnb. To our surprise, people from all over the world, of every sexual orientation, every age and religion come to stay with us. Some want to be left alone, but most want to talk. I often sit in my man cave/deck when I'm home and drink coffee or sip wine. A recent guest, Joe, jokes with me about all the women who want to date him but how time just doesn't allow him to meet this opportunity. I joke back, saying, "I don't remember ever having a problem like that in my dating years!"

Joe opens up, saying, "You know, one-night stands are not all they are cracked up to be. I think you leave a part of your soul with the person and steal part of hers."

I nod. I am listening.

Joe wants to tell me more. "You know, sometimes, I remember her eyes. She wants more—wants to know she's the only one," he pauses. Then Joe confesses, "I feel guilty. Sometimes, I answer their messages but, other times, I ignore them – go on to new hunting grounds. It's sort of an addiction, Al! Once I start, I can't stop!"

"Sorry, Joe," I say.

Joe continues, "You know, you have to keep all your dates in different cities! You don't want them to compare notes or else it gets bad."

"Sorry, Joe," I respond softly.

"Maybe one day I'll find what I'm looking for, Al," as he gets up to leave.

I ask, "Where are you off to, Joe?"

"Oh, I have a date tonight," as he bows and shakes his head.

"Peace on you, Joe," I offer as he goes.

"When I kept silent, my bones wasted away through my groaning all day long. For day and night your hand was heavy on me; my strength was sapped as in the heat of summer" (Psalm 32:3-4).

Release valves

Confessions have weight. They create pressure, like a hot water heater.

I hear creaking and popping noises when I lie in bed. I do what I always do. Ignore it. If I ignore it, it will go away, right? Wrong. It gets worse.

Deb asks, "What's that noise?" I respond, "Eh, it's nothing."

Later on, I trace the noise to our hot water heater. It is old, and I don't know what to do. I call a plumber who says sediment has built up in the bottom of the tank. As water heats over and over again, the minerals separate and collect at the bottom of the tank. On top of this, the plumber says, "The release valve has rusted shut" (Yes, go spray WD-40 on your hot water release valve today!).

I ask, "So, what does all this mean?"

The plumber answers, "You have a rocket ready to take off when it builds up pressure!"

My bed happens to be right above the water heater building pressure underneath in the basement. Now, I'm no rocket scientist, but guess what I did? I replaced the water heater.

Friends, my journey into the *wild* is about listening to souls with pent-up pressure building from life's challenges. Challenges that often trace back fifty years. With no confessor, each soul is like a rusted release valve waiting to explode. The pressure harms many aspects of their life. Sometimes it can turn catastrophic. "When I keep silent about my sin, my bones wasted away through groaning all day long," writes King David in Psalm 32:3.

Jack is one big guy in my bar. I don't think he even realizes it, but he must stand six feet eight inches and about 350 pounds. He scoots around the bar as if he were as average sized as the rest of us! When I come in the bar, Jack often makes a religious joke, "Pastor Al, I walked on water this week!"

"Really, Jack?" I volley back.

"Yeah, but my mom always thinks that!" he says.

Or, "Pastor Al, I did twelve Hail Mary's last week!"

"Really, Jack?"

"Yeah, talking to my brother on the phone, I used fourteen cuss words in one run-on sentence! Was that enough Hail Mary's?" he laughs.

Then there is, "When I was a kid, I had to go to Methodist church three times a week. God, you think I would have learned something or came out believing something," he exclaims.

This time I don't volley back. I wait. I place my hand on Jack's shoulder and ask, "You know the only problem I have with you, Jack?"

"What, Pastor Al?" he replies nervously.

Sensing something, I pivot and offer, "I like you, Jack."

Big Jack softens, "I like you too, Pastor Al." Then he asks, "So will you pray for my daughter?"

"Sure, Jack," I respond.

"She lost her three-year-old child. He just died and we don't know why!" this big man cries. I can barely hold him up. I find myself crying too, "God bless you, Jack." He nods, receiving my blessing.

Do I think confessions with no release valve create stress? I do. Do I believe confessions with no confessor bloc the progress of faith and conversion every person yearns to experience? I do. Do I believe a lifetime of unrelieved hurts, losses, and offences cause mental illness? I do. The *wild*, I suspect has gotten too wild to fit in our systems. But the wild still longs for a confessor to come and stay in their space.

When Jesus hangs on the cross crying out a confession to His confessor, "Why did you forsake me?" (Psalm 22:1) He channels the pent-up pressure of humanity in need of release and opens a way forward for someone who listens to hear, hold, and intercede.

"For I have the desire to do what is good, but I cannot carry it out. For I do not do the good I want to do, but the evil I do not want to do—this I keep on doing" (Romans 7:18-19).

What blocks the Confessor?

What builds up pent-up pressure in our souls? Two images portray the blockage in my soul: an echo chamber in our minds, and an idol in our hearts.

A past narrative of a man I hate loudly echoes in my mind. I am unable to escape the echo chamber of him in my narrative. If I confess I hate him 2,000 times, surely, the pressure releases, right? No. 5,000 times? No.

Now, not every time I am sinned against and sin in response, does it create an echo chamber. There are times when I confess my sin to God alone where the offense does not echo. But the offenses that trip wires of deep wounds in my past echo. When the echo chamber of ways I have been sinned against and sin towards someone builds up pressure in my soul, I need help from another: a confessor.

As I confess my hate, my confessor doesn't correct me, interrupt me, or tell me to repent and get over it. He listens, hears, and holds. Someone with skin, ears, and a face, created in God's image hears me and allows the blockage to lessen and lighten. A confessor listening within my echo chamber *begins* to relieve the pressure. Having a confessor hear my echo chamber clears enough space and lessens the noise in my mind to begin the necessary heart work of loving the one I hate.

The problem is, the heart work feels a lot like death, because it is. It puts to death the idol in my heart. An idol is not always a physical object, although it can be. An idol is also a deep desire I have made into an ultimate desire. It's what my heart believes I need like my body needs oxygen. You see, the man I hate toppled over my idol of acceptance, respect, and significance. Like a child robbed of a precious toy, my soul screams, "mine," and goes after the culprit, setting off the echo chamber.

With my idol toppled and the echo chamber quieted, my heart's affection attaches to Jesus, whose acceptance, value, and significance abound towards me. The emotional wealth I find in

Jesus, helps me stop screaming at the man I hate internally. Refusing to rehearse his offense and exact payment with myself as judge, silences the echo chamber further. I refuse to fondle the memories internally or recount to others his faults. The release valve works. The stress and hate diminish. God takes His place as the righteous judge of the universe in my mind and heart.

Can we find our own *confessor*? It is really the only path to get release from our noisy echo chambers in our minds and idol-worshipping souls. Being a *confessee* is an essential dynamic of becoming a confessor. To "hold space" for others needs the experience of people "holding space" for us.

Final Thoughts

When creation falls from its original perfection, the Great Confessor, God himself, seeks out the man and asks him, "Where are you?" The confessor in the *wild* asks the same question whether using these same words or not. When we enter the confessional space as confessor, can we "wait for it?" May we become aware of the raw, sacred, primitive place of conception where confessions are born and a confessor listens? A confessor steps into this space. It's a space God provides for his dearly loved children to be heard by another living soul, whose listening is a sign of God's healing love.

The space of a Confessor ... How did I miss this?

Chapter 2: History of the Confessor

The Green Mile is a 1996 novel by Stephen King written in the voice of prison guard Paul Edgecomb; it was made into a movie three years later as Edgecomb narrates his strange experiences with death row inmates in 1935. While time ticks toward each man's execution date, unsettling and fantastic surprises unfold. One inmate possesses a superpower.

John Coffey is a huge hulk of a man but childlike. He has the miraculous ability to locate others' diseases and sins and take them into his own body. And he can see hidden evils. Officer Percy, a despised guard, abuses prisoners. Coffey sees deep evil in Percy's soul. He listens, hears, and holds what he discovers.

Coffey is in prison for the murder of two girls. Police found him at the scene, a jury pronounced him guilty, and a judge sentenced him to death. He was not their killer. Having come upon their bodies, he tried to resurrect them but fails.

Officer Edgecomb is the first person in the prison to experience Coffey's healing power. Coffey ingests Edgecombe's chronic bladder infection into himself, and Edgecombe is healed.

The prison warden's wife is terminally ill. Edgecomb arranges for Coffey to come to the warden's home. Coffey approaches his wife lying in her bed, ingests her illness into himself, so she is healed. With her debilitating disease in him, Coffey needs assistance walking out of the house.

Awed by Coffey's healing powers, Edgecomb volunteers to help the falsely indicted, childlike giant escape from prison. But Coffey has ingested the confessions and diseases of so many condemned people, he is ready to be free of this cruel world. He insists on facing his execution. When Coffey is strapped to the electric chair, Edgecomb shakes the prisoner's hand and thanks him for his life and apparent supernatural mission.

Sin-Eaters

John Coffey's mysterious gift points to a confessor's ability, inexplicable, sometimes mystical, to understand and ingest human tragedy and offenses. This reminds me of the phenomenon of the eighteenth and early nineteenth century called the "Sin-Eater."

"For if you forgive other people when they sin against you, your heavenly Father will also forgive you" (Matthew 6:14).

Keith Veronese, in *The Weird but True Stories about Sin Eaters* (2013), writes of this European practice.

> Sin Eaters … had a very singular role within some segments of Christianity. Sin Eaters performed a ceremony

wherein they took on the sins that the deceased performed – sins that went unforgiven or without confession prior to death. People typically hired a Sin Eater in situations where the deceased died unexpectedly. By consuming bread and a drink (usually wine or beer) placed on, or ritually waved over, the dead body, onlookers believed the dead person's sins were digested by the eater after he or she consumed this beggar's feast.

In time, Sin Eaters would also attend to those who had died of natural causes. People believed the ritual helped prevent the dead from wandering the countryside after death. The Sin Eater would receive a small payment and a scant meal. No amount of money, however, could overcome the social stigma connected to a Sin Eater's line of work. Neither could it make up for the poverty and solitude in which most Sin-Eaters lived. Each village typically had its "own" Sin-Eater, and the villagers believed this individual would become more and more horrible with each and every ceremony.

Yes, confessions have weight.

The practice of sin-eating was not sanctioned by the Church. The notion that a Sin-Eater could cure anyone's sins was considered heresy, despite the practice secretly persisting.

The 1926 book *Funeral Customs* by Bertram S. Puckle mentions the Sin-Eater.

Professor Evans of Presbyterian College, Carmarthen, actually saw a sin-eater about the year 1825, who was then living near Llanwenog, Cardiganshire. Abhorred by the superstitious villagers as a thing unclean, the sin-eater cut himself off from all social intercourse with his fellow creatures by reason of the life he had chosen; he lived as a rule in a remote place by himself, and those who chanced to meet him avoided him as they would a leper. This unfortunate soul was held to be the associate of evil spirits, and given to witchcraft, incantations and unholy practices; only when a death took place did they seek him out, and when his purpose was accomplished they burned the wooden bowl and platter from which he had eaten the food handed across, or placed on the corpse for his consumption.

The Sin-Eater underscores what many cultures, religions, and civilizations recognize as "sacred space" inside every soul: a space where thoughts, offenses, hopes, and expressions of faith happen. For many, whether unintentionally or deliberately, like the Sin-Eater, this space gets filled with sins and hurts. When these experiences are unexpressed, a soul gets heavy and weighed down. The conscience is a careful record keeper. Sins and hurts begin like a small tropical depression, but, when left alone, become a Category 5 hurricane later in life. Our body and soul do not hold unconfessed offenses well. Confessions are constantly, desperately looking for release, release facilitated by a confessor.

"Now I rejoice in what I am suffering for you, and I fill up in my flesh what is still lacking in regard to Christ's afflictions" (Colossians 1:24).

History's Confessors

History is a confession looking for a confessor.

Why do we have historians? History needs confessors. Past events, experiences, and people hide for ten, one-hundred, or one-thousand years, or more.

Historians, archeologists, scientists, and writers continuously make discoveries from the past, revealing both tragedy and advancement. Recently, archaeologists in Japan discovered its largest dinosaur skeleton yet, a duck-billed creature named *Kamuysaurus Japonicus*. Researchers are finding the places the dinosaur lived, what it ate, and how it became extinct. The earth gives up its secrets from thousands and thousands of years ago and allows us to find them.

One of history's secrets is sunken slave trade ships, which continue to be discovered on the ocean's floor. Scuba divers find hidden tombs in overcrowded hulls full of shackles and human bones. The Smithsonian Institution takes a lead role in the Slave Works Project. Diver, Michael Cottman, relates his work in his book *Shackles From the Deep*. How many more of the generally accepted ten to twelve-million slaves transported across the Atlantic Ocean may be located remains to be seen. By some accounts over 12,000 ships made more than 40,000 voyages over two-hundred and fifty years. These newly discovered sunken ships are once-forgotten memorials, naturally preserved for hundreds of years.

History tells stories of Confessors hearing confessions.

St. John Vianney, born May 8, 1786 in Dardilly, France to devout Christian parents, is one of history's best-known confessors. In 1790, an anticlerical phase of the French revolution forced many priests into hiding. During this time, the Vianney family hid priests who could administer the sacraments of the church in secret. Young John Vianney began to see the rogue priests as heroes as he practiced his faith in secret.

In 1809, after being drafted into Napoleon's army, Vianney escaped and eventually found himself in the village of Les Noes, where deserters gathered. He changed his name to Jerome Vincent and opened a school for children. The following year, deserters were given amnesty, freeing him to attend seminary at Verrieres-en-Forez.

In 1818, Vianney received an appointment to be a parish priest. In this sacred calling he encouraged the people to confess their sins. Vianney heard confessions for as many as eighteen hours a day! He became so well-respected, people from all over the world came to his confessional booth. Thirty-seven years later Vianney was hearing the confessions of twenty-thousand people a year (John Vianney, 2004).

I do not tell the story of John Vianney to argue for the Roman Catholic church's confessional booth. But it is a picture of the power of confession. People need someone to whom they can tell what's heavy in their soul, but not simply to anyone. As with Vianney, the confessor is a human instrument through whom spirit and flesh commune. The transforming power of the exchange between *confessee* and confessor does for the soul what a blood transfusion accomplishes for a depleted and diseased body. Perhaps all of Christ's church needs to revive, honor, and protect this sacred practice.

Three hundred years before Vianney, a German Augustinian monk launched a spiritual and intellectual transformation of Christianity and hence the broader culture too. Martin Luther's awakening to the grace of God moved him to protest the religious status quo. His rejection of key theological precepts so threatened the Church that he was condemned for heresy. Have an issue with a detractor? Brand him a heretic or infidel to get him out of the way. Many of his contemporaries wanted Luther burned at the stake.

Although Luther challenged many fundamental practices and traditions of the Church, he did not advocate its overthrow. Instead, he sought its reformation. Among those things he upheld was the sacrament of confession, the ancient practice of the confessional where penitents received the gift of God's forgiveness when they made their confessions to the priest.

In his 1529 Catechism, Luther praised confession before a pastor, or fellow Christian, to receive absolution, the forgiveness of sins. Luther taught confession has two parts: the confession of the parishioner and the absolution given by the confessor. He defended the practice and grace of confession based on two principal scriptures (John Vianney, 2004).

> Therefore confess your sins to each other and pray for each other so that you may be healed. The prayer of a righteous person is powerful and effective (James 5:16). And with that he [Jesus] breathed on them and said, "Receive the Holy Spirit. If you forgive anyone's sins, their sins are forgiven; if you do not forgive them, they are not forgive (John 20:22-23).

Although there is no agreement among Christians about whether confession should be considered a sacrament, Luther, among others, readily acknowledged the human need to tell someone what weighs heavily on the soul.

Protesting Protestants

Luther took profound exception to long-held beliefs and traditions preserved by the hierarchy of the Church. The impact of his effort to reform the Church continues even today. Some in the Protestant churches tend to lead with their inherited "protesting muscle." Because Protestants seldom stop talking there's little room left for the flexing of our "confessor muscle." Are we who are descended from the movement set in motion by Luther so used to objecting that we've fallen into the rut of speaking before listening, of answering questions people are not asking? Have we become noisy gongs who drown out the cries of souls who care nothing about theological orthodoxy but who do want to be known, heard, understood, and loved? (Zucker and Harris, 2010)

In my Presbyterian tribe, we put great emphasis on "credentialing." It can be a world of investigation and dissection that is devoid of understanding the dynamics of life in the *wild*. What I see is, our young ministers, once ordained, make their way into the world repeating the same credentialing process. They try to impose theological orthodoxy – what they believe to be the correct understanding and beliefs – on the experiences of those around them. They lose touch with the *wild*. Our ministers are not evangelizing but are *truthing* the non-Christian world at arm's length. Meanwhile, non-Christian people have so much pent-up frustration about the Church's deafness to the authentic cries of the soul, they are no longer listening. Is it any wonder few people in the *wild* are entering the confines of the average church?

The role of the confessor is *not* to replace God's redemptive power in His Son Jesus, but to be an empowered servant of God who is willing to wade into the *wild* – the spaces where most people live. The confessor receives the confessions of the soul and points the *confessee* to God and Christ when he or she is ready.

The confessor is a critical role for the minister who seeks a parish in the *wild*. Again, I am using parish as a place where people gather and know each other. The *wild* is outside church walls and church culture. People in the *wild* have confessions in need of a confessor. The *wild* is waiting for someone to be present, to choose to come back often, to adopt a parish and be adopted by a parish. Many ordained ministers do not realize it, but this may just be what we have always longed for!

How do we accomplish this? Begin to listen, hear, and hold. Watch for healing and faith to stir. The way into the current world we find ourselves in – this *wild* frontier – is not as a *truther, teller, presenter* to strangers. Rather, our way into the *wild* is as a confessor available to hear others' confessions. People in the *wild*, no matter their belief system, need a listener. Everyone longs for a listener, a hearer, and a holder of their hurts, hopes, and questions. The confessor is there to intercede for the *confessee* until healing and faith stir.

"Therefore, holy brothers and sisters, who share in the heavenly calling, fix your thoughts on Jesus, whom we acknowledge as our apostle and high priest" (Hebrews 3:1).

Final Thoughts

I am still a weekend carpenter, having put myself through college and grad school as a licensed home builder. As I near sixty years old, I build things differently. Now, this aging weekend carpenter is building things to last, not merely for five or ten years, but a lifetime. I use stainless steel screws and Gorilla Glue. I attach boards with the direction of the wood grains in mind. I build things which will now outlast me. It has taken a lifetime to learn how to build things that will last.

Similarly, as the days ahead shorten, I think about and do evangelism differently. In the past I evangelized by talking, truthing, and presenting. Now, I build by listening, hearing, and holding. This confessor path into the *wild* follows a different beat than most brick- and-mortar pastors.

I see history, including Biblical history, as a confession looking for a confessor. In the Garden of Eden, when God walks with the woman and the man, what words did they share? What did silence do for the relationship? What questions arose from Adam's heart? Eve's? When the known world falls from glory to evil, God, the Confessor, pursues His shame-filled creatures, asking the ancient question: "Where are you?" (Genesis 3:9). God, as Confessor, in His kind pursuit, listens and hears.

"Where are you?" is the raw, starting point of a confessor hearing a confession. History shows the need of a confessor. And the need for the confessor is growing in our time and space today.

The Confessor in history ... How did I miss this?

Chapter 3: The Tattoo Artist

The confessions of our time and space, tattoos, are looking for their Confessor. It appears the proliferation of tattoos is being used to call out the confessors of our age. When the soul starts running out of words, it "inks" art on its wrapper.

Al Dayhoff, author)

I dreamed a dream. I watched the TV series *Lost in Space* (1965-1968) in my formative years, and I still dream within this show.

I am riding on a SpaceX rocket visiting a planet outside our solar system. As the rocket lands on the Mars-like planet, the stairway lowers to the surface. I walk down, and aliens on this planet greet me. The creatures appear human-like, almost like my middle-school self, with one major difference – all have pictures, writings, and designs all over their skin. These markings appear permanent.

Whenever I speak, the aliens point to a picture or design on their skin. I have no idea what they are saying, but the aliens persist in showing me their marks. Why won't they use words? I realize I must learn this way of communicating because I cannot understand them. And just when I think I understand, my judgmental spirit causes their marks to glow, blink, and decoy me. Consequently, these alien beings do not trust me and leave me alone. As I move about the planet on my own, I observe small temples with priests who create these markings. Each person and priest collaborate to design a unique, permanent mark – a seemingly sacramental exchange on this alien planet. *Such a silly dream, eh?*

When I wake up, I realize I am living on *this* planet. It isn't a dream.

In a coffee shop in Sanur, Indonesia, I stand behind a woman with numbers tattooed on her arm – 238,900 x 2 = 477,800. Getting her attention, I say, "Your tattoo is interesting! Does it have a story?"

"Yes," she says as she turns back around.

I wait. Respectful silence often pays.

She turns back to answer, "My mom used to say, 'I love you to the moon and back!' It helps me every day." Her number tattoo "calculates the math between earth and the moon" for her mother's love every day.

> "Can a mother forget the baby at her breast and have no compassion on the child she has borne? Though she may forget, I will not forget you! See, I have engraved you on the palms of my hands; your walls are ever before me" (Isaiah 49:15-16).

Tattoos

Sometimes, confessions become tattoos. We now live on a planet where, in the West, many people write secrets and stories in permanent ink on their skin. Around 3,600 tattoo conventions gather across our planet annually where thousands upon thousands shop for an artist who will *ink* them on site. At the time I write, the tattoo industry in the United States generates over one billion dollars each year. Is this a fad, a movement, or a phenomenon? Whatever one calls it, the tattoo industry shows no sign of slowing down.

Many inside the church miss the connection between tattoos and confessions. For too long, I did. But in my blues bar, I can no longer ignore them. Seeing the bar as my parish enables me to see a tattoo and discover a confession.

The lady sitting at the bar embodies sadness as she leans into her drink. I ask her, "Does your tattoo have a story?"

She looks at me like I am lost in space! She slurs, "All of them."

I wait.

Eventually, she explains, "I counsel Special Forces soldiers with PTSD. Each tattoo is a soldier I've counseled who has taken his own life. This week another suicide ... with a client I became romantically involved with ... so, I'm thinking about getting one for him."

I am silent. The shock of her confession is like a body blow to my heart. I feel her sadness more deeply.

Let me explain. After spending nineteen years starting a church, growing a church, and building a grand church building, I looked out at the full congregation and realized that these people are all from other struggling churches nearby. Maybe I am a little slow, but in all the starting, growing and building, I missed what was happening. But all of a sudden, it hits me! I know what my next one thousand conversations are going to be, and I do not want to be in those conversations any longer. I love my people, but I am convinced there must be something more than walking on Christian carpet answering Christian questions every day. Do I want to invest the last trimester of my ministry this way? No.

"Then the Lord put a mark on Cain so that no one who found him would kill him" (Genesis 4:15).

Tattoo Confessions

I head to a Blues Bar to try to find my way forward and, to my own amazement, I never leave. Yet, I did leave the brick-and-mortar church (Dayhoff, 2017). Now, I am Pastor Al to over five hundred people who frequent the bar. They make me cry. I am theirs, and they are mine -- people from all walks of life who are my friends, curiosity-seekers, and parish members. I hope my journey of discovery with them never ends.

Do confessions hide underneath tattoos? I was looking for confessions in a journal, a poem, or in a pastor's office, while tattoos were right in front of me. When I first noticed them, I began to find an entrance to a person's soul. Discovering confessions under a tattoo caught me unaware. But not anymore.

After conducting more than 5,000 tattoo interviews, I stumble upon the first one that looks silly, a bag of Skittles tattooed on a young woman's neck. My first thought is, "Why does this young woman want Skittles tattooed on her neck for the next fifty to sixty years?" I walk up to her and lie, "I like your tattoo!"

Silence. It never bothers me to wait for the response, because once the owner of the tattoo looks underneath it, memories, people, forgotten lovers, and subconscious wounds begin to come out. But this time she pauses so long that even I feel awkward.

I say, "I'm a tattoo researcher. Does your tattoo have a story?"

Looking me in the eyes, she answers, "The last time I saw my father alive, he threw me a bag of Skittles."

Oh, my! The air goes out of my judgmental soul. I am grateful to hear such a sacred and weighty confession.

Tattoostoryhunters is a Facebook page of a team of researchers who search for sacred spaces, make discoveries, and learn more about the role of the confessor. In August of 2018, our research team sponsored a booth on Main Street at The Sturgis Motorcycle Rally in South Dakota. Ten minister-researchers joined me for ten days at the world's largest motorcycle gathering, where 600,000 bikers attend.

Great idea, huh? What could go wrong?

We put up a large banner across the top of our booth that reads, "Does your tattoo have a story?" We set out the book, *Tattoos: Telling the Secrets of the Soul.* But we are there to listen, because the tattoo owner needs to talk, no matter how intimidating he or she might appear. As you might imagine, we encountered scores of intimidating figures. Some passed by a first time with menacing looks. When they walked by a second time, we figured they might say or do something. Yet as the week went on, more and more softened in their demeanor, introduced themselves, and began to tell their tattoo stories. In the end, bikers crowded all around telling their tattoo stories.

The most common tattoo we find at the Sturgis rally is a tombstone. Today's new cemetery is on skin. We now live in a time and space where tombstones are walking before us every day.

Sturgis bike rally, 2018

Three Small Hearts

Traveling back from Sturgis, Dan, one of our researchers, tells this story.

While driving home, my head, neck and shoulders hurt. So, I take a pit stop for some ibuprofen and caffeine. A dirty and deserted-looking convenience store is the only option I see, so I pull in. I grab a Mountain Dew Voltage (don't judge!), Ibuprofen, and approach the counter. The tattoos of the checkout clerk are visible across her arms, neck, and face.

I say, "I like your tattoos. I'll bet there's a story or two behind them."

"Yes, there is," she replies. Then silence.

Truthfully, I am ready to get back to driving. But I try a different approach. I ask whether she has a Facebook account and find out that she does. I tell her to look up our Tattoo Storyhunters page to see our adventures in Sturgis with bikers. This opens the door for the stories behind the tattoos on her arms.

Then, she slowly points to three small hearts under her right eye. Pointing to the first one, she says with a smile, "This one is for my daughter." As she points to the next two, her smile disappears. She quietly explains, "And I lost a set of twins."

Time stops. Finally, I respond, "I'm so sorry."

She replies, "That's OK. It's been a while and it's easier to talk about now."

I am feeling sorrow, sympathy, confusion, amazement, but I simply say, "Thank you for sharing, and God bless you."

Tattoos are sacred space. They are spring-loaded: you touch one with your finger, with a question, and it begins to vibrate, seeking a listener. The longer the tattoo talks, the more depth and spirituality comes flowing out of the person.

Heat Sink

A heat sink enables circuit boards to work. When engineers make a circuit board for a computer, phone or satellite, heat is their opponent. Electrons racing through a wire, gold or titanium produce heat causing the whole system to break down. The heat sink is a physical component drawing off the heat, thus allowing the circuit to work as it is designed.

In an age of trauma, tattoos function as heat sinks. While tattoos contain a story of a wound, the art continues interpreting life and its joys, confusions, and broken hearts. Tattoos tell a soul's story. When the artist inks and cuts out the skin, the tattoo becomes a physical heat sink, drawing the heat away enough for a soul to keep thinking, introspecting, and discovering.

As a confessor learns to listen, he or she becomes a heat sink of sorts as well. Listening to hear and hearing to hold a confession draws off the heat, so that a person's soul may function as designed.

Tattoos hold secrets or layers of stories underneath them. Many people get a new tattoo over an old one if they no longer like the design. I suspect, sometimes, the person wants a new anonymity because too many people discover the tattoo's secret.

Discovery

Some tattoos withhold their secrets from the owner for many years. Tattoo designs are birthed from both the conscious and the subconscious. During an interview, the confessor will often witness a discovery take place. As the owner speaks the story out loud, he or she often ventures into uncharted territory.

Adam and I met in the Ka' Tiki Blues Bar, located near St. Petersburg, Florida. He was a regular in this dive bar that many call their home. Shirts are optional at Ka' Tiki, so I could see Looney Tune tattoos -- Tom and Jerry, the Road Runner, Yosemite Sam, Daffy Duck, Porky Pig, Elmer Fudd, Tweety Bird, and Sylvester the Cat—and these were just the ones on his back. His arms displayed the Tasmanian Devil, Speedy Gonzales, and Wile E. Coyote. On his thighs were Bugs Bunny and Foghorn Leghorn. With each beer Adam more enthusiastically recounted his favorite stories from the different cartoons inked on his body.

I ask, "How much money have you invested in all these tattoos?"

"About $14K," he replies.

"So, why?" I ask.

"Why not? What could be better than a tattoo, man?" Fueled by five beers, he laughs off my question.

I say, "Thank you for the tour," and wait.

After a long pause, Adam comments, "I guess when your old man kills himself when you are eight, you write the happy things you did together, huh?"

Trudy, his favorite bartender, takes the empty beer from his grip and helps him hold another beer, number six.

Figuring it was time to go, I tell him, "It was an honor to get to know your dad."

He shakes his head acknowledging my words and turns back toward Trudy.

Tattoos in Biblical Perspective

Tattoos are an armor of sorts, a strange mix of self-protection and self-exposure. Is this a sign the soul subconsciously knows it needs armor for life's battles? I think so.

The Apostle Paul describes the armor of God in Ephesians 6:1-20. Spiritual armor enables followers of Christ to do spiritual warfare in their souls and in the souls of others. Each piece of spiritual armor describes either a trait or tool of faith for the Christian. In short, they tell a story.

When a Christian confessor is spiritually equipped, he or she may skillfully hear what the tattoo armor seeks to both protect and reveal. Tattoos originate in the direction of seeking protection. Yet, whether knowingly or not, the tattoo is also an expression of its owner's very soul and an entry point for the confessor into this spiritual realm. As the Spirit of God is telling the person, "Your struggle is not against flesh and blood but against spiritual forces of evil" (Ephesians 6:11).

"The belt of truth buckled around your waist" (Ephesians 6:14a) reminds me of a particular kind of tattoo called a "tramp stamp." I recoil at the name, but it is a tattoo a woman often puts at the bottom of her back, just above the waist of her jeans. But the slang term does her an injustice because most of the time, I hear a woman talking about her beauty. This tattoo says, "I am designed uniquely and beautifully." I suspect this truth is an intrinsic characteristic of women mirroring the Image of God.

"The breastplate of righteousness" (Ephesians 6:14b) makes me remember my friend Cory with a tattoo NO REGRETS across his chest. Skulls, flowers, and vines intersect with the two words. I ask him about it. He replies, "It's obvious! Why do you need to overthink my tattoo? I live with no regrets," ending with a long pause seemingly full of regrets. I suspect he has many regrets and is looking for some armor to free him from the troubling whispers in the night.

"Your feet fitted with the gospel of peace" (Ephesians 6:15a) prompts my memory of a tattoo on my friend Rhonda's lower leg. The lyrics of John Lennon's 1971 song, "Imagine," spiral around her leg. She sees herself as a messenger with a song of peace and wholeness in our world, but I sense she is lacking wholeness on the inside.

"Take up the shield of faith" (Ephesians 6:16) speaks of hope and belief in a protector who watches over each person. As Jimmy says, he has the "ghosts of his father, grandfather, and great grandfather" tattooed on his arm and shoulder. He believes their ghosts walk the earth alongside him, watching over him, giving him advice, and reminding him they are proud of him.

All of these are signs that the soul wants to confess its hopes, dreams, and failures. Tattoos are like a buoy floating on the surface of the skin but tethered to a wound or desire in their soul. It longs to be discovered, known, cleansed, and loved.

Often, in response to my tattoo research, I receive emails from Christians quoting, "Do not put tattoos on your skin" (Leviticus 19:28). I get it. Yet the cultural background of this command is the association of tattoos with ancestor worship. (Admittedly, Jimmy's tattoos get into this realm to some degree.) However, in the biblical narrative, God writes on skin. God gives Cain a mark on his skin after he murders his brother Abel (Genesis 4). This mark somehow protects Cain from vengeance from others. God commands Abraham and his descendants to circumcise their sons as a sign of God's promise. Isaiah says of God's heart, "Behold I have inscribed you on the palms of my hands" (Isaiah 49:16). One day Jesus will return with "King of Kings and Lord of Lords" written on his thigh (Revelation 19:16).

Tattoo Artists

As a result of discovering confessions underneath tattoos, my respect for the tattoo artist has grown enormously. I interview them now frequently.

Since most people are no longer willing to tell a priest or pastor their secrets, they must look elsewhere for a confessor. Many people have chosen to share their secrets with the tattoo artist. The bond between the tattooed person and the artist is a priestly or shaman-like relationship. The tattoo artist sits, listens, and interprets the messages coming from deep within his client. The artist has earned the right to hear, interpret, and form how the confession appears.

In 1880, Auguste Rodin received a commission for a statue as a piece of a larger work, *The Gates of Hell*. Rodin's inspiration was Dante's *The Divine Comedy*. The sculptor chiseled a man sitting on a rock with his chin resting on one hand, deep in thought. Originally titled *The Poet*, today the world knows this famous image as *The Thinker*. For many, this statue represents Dante at the Gates of Hell pondering his massive poem, *Inferno*. Dante's epic poem chronicles his imaginary journey through Hell. The *Inferno* consists of nine concentric circles of torment – the dwelling of the violent, selfish, and fraudulent. The poem portrays a soul's journey toward and away from God (Gates of Hell, 2004).

Today's tattoo artist is like this poet of old. The tattoo artist who stays in his or her craft comes to be the "thinker at the gate" of the human soul. Tattoos become poetic in their imagery, a joint expression by the owner of the tattoo and in part by the artist who listens, hears, holds, and inks. The artist and this client often form a bond that lasts a lifetime because the artist hears the secrets and portrays them permanently on his *confessee* – a confession finding a confessor. Confessions from the inside rise to the surface of the skin in permanent ink.

Sometimes, tattoo artists who have practiced their craft for many years become darkened and weighed down by the unspeakable pain shared in the studio over many hours by many people. They are like Dante contemplating hell. The pain, blood, and wincing of receiving a tattoo elicits pain from within the artist's own soul. The space they enter is sacred, the act of inking almost sacramental. As confessor, the tattoo artist listens for somewhere between thirty minutes and thirty years to the secrets of the soul.

My friend, Bob, is a seasoned tattoo artist at the Lucky 13 Tattoo Studio in Richmond, Virginia. A military veteran, Bob studies philosophy, wears black leather that matches his motorcycle, and was tattooed before tattoos were common. He is living his dream being a tattoo artist. Like most artists, Bob is creative, passionate about his craft, and sensitive to his clients. The more clients come, the more he grows as a listener, shaman, and soul doctor. He enters his clients' wrestling about what image to put where.

Bob knows that even a whimsical tattoo may be a trap door into the deepest parts of the soul where pain, abandonment, and hope hide. Tattoos form in the vault of a person's soul. He experiences the Image of God so desperate to talk, it writes on its wrapper in permanent ink. The spiritual art of confessions, where the church was once strong, has now re-appeared with tattoo artists. Bob hears and holds confessions that long to be heard.

"Panther" is one of Bob's returning clients and a close friend. Bob and Panther plan on attending each other's funeral, whoever goes first. Panther is a retired Army sniper. No one sees him when he comes or leaves. As with a panther, you only know he was there if there is a kill. Because panthers kill quietly and quickly, they are mysterious creatures.

Panther has seven panthers tattooed on his body. Each one tells a story he is unfolding and processing from the vault of his soul. Each panther marks a kill. Although Panther's victims never saw him, they remain vivid in him. His tattoos have questions underneath them: Was that kill necessary? Conversely, did the shot not taken result in too many other deaths? Was there a child or civilian killed by landmines meant for or planted by American soldiers?

Panther and Bob allow me to observe their ritual. I am privy to their sacred space. These two friends do not need to talk to hear what the other is thinking. Fewer words give more space for experiencing the gift of being together. Yet, as Bob inks, Panther speaks of the pain inflicted by the ink gun. At the end of the session, Panther says, "Thanks. I'll be 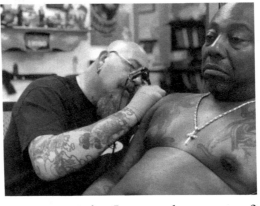 back," as he offers a generous tip. I sense the power of a Tattoo Confessor hearing unspoken confessions deep from the soul but marked on the skin.

I watch Panther get in a black Chevy Suburban with blackened windows. As he drives away, I think of the pain and blood from the new tattoo getting acquainted with its owner and fellow panther tattoos.

"The purposes of a person's heart are deep waters, but one who has insight draws them out" (Proverbs 20:5).

Final Thoughts

How did I miss this when tattoos were right before my eyes?

The *wild* is full of confessions looking for a confessor. In our time and place, tattoo artists have stepped up to listen, hear, and hold what the soul speaks. Then, they craft an ink confession on the canvas of the skin. Maybe Christians in the *wild* can find a way to step into this sacred space like tattoo artists. Many people who gave up on our churches will still share their tattoo story in the *wild* with someone who will listen. *"Hi, nice ink. Does your tattoo have a story?"*

How did I miss this? Tattoos are confessions seeking a confessor.

Chapter 4: The Priest Confessor

Marvel Comics' Daredevil animates the inner life of a superhero.

Matt Murdock grows up in Hell's Kitchen in New York City. Matt's father, Battlin' Jack Murdock, is murdered, leaving Matt an orphan. One day, Matt pushes a man out of the way of a reckless truck, and a radioactive substance falls from the truck, blinding Matt. While he can no longer see, the radioactive substance increases all his other senses to superhuman strength. He grows up to fight criminals through his day job as a lawyer, but, by night, he becomes Daredevil.

Daredevil's four superhuman powers are taste, touch, smell, and hearing. His taste allows him to identify every ingredient in a recipe. His touch enables him to read by feeling ink from a printed page. His smell identifies everyone by their scent. His hearing reaches heartbeats, whispers, and hidden confessions. He walks through the world hearing the secrets of the human heart. He hears and distinguishes when a heart is lying, plotting evil, or running scared.

Yet even Daredevil's superpowers do not allow him to be his own confessor. In the 2015 Daredevil series, Matt returns to his childhood priest.

> *Matt Murdock*: I'm not asking for forgiveness for what I've done, Father. I'm asking for forgiveness for what I'm about to do.
>
> *Father Lantom:* That's not how this works.
>
> *Matt Murdock:* Do you believe in the Devil, Father?
>
> *Father Lantom:* You mean . . . as a concept?
>
> *Murdock*: No. Do you believe he exists? In this world, among us?
>
> *Father Lantom:* You want the short answer or the long one
>
> *Murdock:* Just the truth.

Father Lantom answers by relating a tale from his missionary days in Rwanda, concluding at last, "I saw the Devil. So yes, Matthew, I believe he walks among us... taking many forms" (Daredevil, 2004).

"Every high priest is selected from among the people and is appointed to represent the people in matters related to God, to offer gifts and sacrifices for sins. He can deal gently with those who are ignorant and are going astray, since he himself is subject to weakness (Hebrews 5:1-2).

Today's Priests

In our day, most priests are hidden inside a building, a book, a meeting, or a Sunday service (coming every three or so days, or so it feels). The priests' space and rhythm dwell in this building. My generation teaches the current generation, "If you can just preach a better sermon, add the right amount of scholarship, wit, and humor, people will come to your building." The people come – but, most often, from other churches.

Recently, I replied to a pastor-friend who acknowledged my work with the "marginal communities" in my parish, saying. My response? We are now *that* marginal community.

Church friends, the Christian community is *not* the dominant culture in the Western world anymore. Instead, Christian influence is diminishing. The dominant culture sees the evangelical Christian community as completely out of touch. How do we respond? Is the priest, pastor, or minister even a presence anymore in the public square?

My faith tribe emphasizes explaining the gospel. In this view, my job, as a minister, is to proclaim, and, if a person doesn't believe, move on. My job is to present the faith proposal for the non-Christian in a compelling manner and invite a response at the end of my proposal. If they do not believe, I, at least, have the satisfaction of knowing their blood is not on my hands. We, over and over again, play the "short game" as the long game take a different system.

Indeed, proclaiming, explaining, and telling are a part of the biblical mandate. Yet the biblical narrative also includes being still, listening, and really hearing. Indeed, silence is one of God's favorite tools for proclaiming!

In John 8:2-11, a woman who had been caught in the act of adultery was dragged before Jesus and accused by the Pharisees. Jesus knew it was a trap; instead of saying a word, he stooped down and started doodling in the dirt. After challenging the Pharisees with their own sin, he went back to drawing in the dirt. Eventually, he looked up and all were gone except the woman. Jesus' act of silent grace led to the forgiveness, restoration, and wholeness of the woman.

Maybe, like the Pharisees, our need to speak comes from our own sense of superiority. We function as if, "When someone believes, they receive the Image of God and have value." However, in my journey of discovering the role of the confessor, I find the Image of God is active and alive in the heart of every non-Christian.

Pain, fear, abandonment, and loss regularly come into conflict with a sense of justice and goodness imprinted on each soul by our Creator. Questions, hurts, hunches, fears, and hopes swirl in the backstory of peoples' minds. Only in a relationship of trust can the soul unburden itself. For years, my sense of superiority resulted in my missing out on relationships with people. Now, I discover relating is how I remain a part of a person's process of believing.

Years ago, while in seminary, I received a phone call. My brother's five-year-old son died in a car accident. Feeling life drain from me, I threw all my seminary books in the trash. I shouted to God, "What kind of a spineless bully would do this to a child?" When I went to the funeral and saw the little, white casket, tears flowed for my nephew and my brother's family. Worse, my brother and sister-in-law are in tears.

Many people in my bar bear the unspeakable wound of losing a child. A blues bar is one place people go to grieve with fellow pilgrims, suspending their minds, listening to a song, getting a few drinks, and dancing all night.

A few years ago, a woman in my bar heard someone say, "That's pastor Al!" Turning, she asks me, "Why are *you* here?"

I answer, "I like Blues music! My name is Al."

"Don't you have better things to do than come here with people who don't care about religion anymore? There are not many religious people here," she argues.

Her eyes say, "Please talk to me," but her tone says, "Please go away." It's as if her left hand signals "Stop" while her right-hand signals, "Come closer, please."

This is the space of the priest-confessor. A priest learns how to be still enough to allow a confession to find its way out. So, I wait, not disagreeing with her or forming a reply. I stand still and watch space open.

A little louder than a whisper, she asks, "What have I done wrong to lose my son?"

I shut my eyes and bow. I feel the pain in her question. I reply, "I am sorry."

She cries. I suspect she has been crying for many years in many places.

Months pass with many conversations with Lucy. Lucy and I talk about faith, her son, and the after-life when she wants. In parish ministry there is no rush to get a soul converted and into a membership class. A natural rhythm develops in this relationship. I am hers, and she is mine. Is my hope to see her come to a saving knowledge of Jesus? Of course, but it must be at her speed for it to be real.

Many who say, "Pastor Al, I cannot believe the whole God, Jesus, and Bible thing." Often, I say, "It's okay! Let me believe for you." I am letting these dear ones know faith incubates. We will know it when it comes. In the meantime, I want each to know she or he is valuable to me and to God. We wrestle through faith together at the right speed and time. People get converted when they do.

"My dear children, for whom I am again in the pains of childbirth until Christ is formed in you" (Galatians 4:19).

The Hitchhiker's Guide to the Galaxy and The Babble fish

The Hitchhiker's Guide to the Galaxy is a science fiction series about Arthur Dent, the last surviving man from earth (made into a movie in 2005). As Arthur travels the galaxy, he carries with him a "Babble Fish," a yellow device energized by the brainwaves of nearby beings. The Babble Fish intercepts all things subconscious in one being and transfers knowledge to its carrier. This device enables Arthur to understand any language and to hear everyone's deepest questions, struggles, or suspicions.

The confessor is like Arthur Dent with the Babble Fish. The confessor listens for the deepest questions, struggles, or suspicions in another's soul. Silence and observation are the confessor's friends. Silence in a confessor's soul offers space for another to speak. In essence, the confessor has a Babble Fish-like power enabling him to say, if he chooses, "I have room for your words … even the ones you don't know you're saying." The confessor discerns what a soul is trying to get out – a confession of sin, pain, hope, or an offense (*Hitchhiker's Guide*, 2001).

When a *confessee* suspects the confessor can hear and understand what he is saying, something mystical happens. Is this a spiritual gift? Is this like the mystery of a sacrament? Is this the Holy Spirit? Yes, maybe.

As the Spirit of God hovers in the play of Creation, so the Spirit plays in the process of new creations. The Holy Spirit indeed fills the Christian confessor and calls the *confessee*, resulting in regeneration and faith. Yet most often, the process takes much longer than the time it takes to read Romans 8:28-30. Add in a person's experience, it probably will not progress in a linear fashion as you enter as confessor. But the pressure is *not* on you, the confessor! God's Spirit is at work before you and is active, hovering, playing, and guiding the process.

It can happen with someone the confessor meets for the first time. It often deepens with continuous presence. A confessor learns to discern the ways another soul wrestles and heals. The *confessee* responds to being understood rather than judged, to hearing words of hope rather than being condemned. Faith and healing begin to stir in the exchange. Consequently, the confessor becomes fiercely protective of the *confessee*. He or she allows each person to be where they are and to take steps of faith – including questions and confessions – as the *confessee* is ready.

"Anyone who listens to the Word but does not do what it says is like someone who looks at his face in a mirror and after looking at

himself goes away and immediately forgets what he looks at"
(James 1:23).

The Three Mirrors

As priest-confessors like Daredevil, we must not fall into the
delusion of thinking we do not need confessors ourselves. No one
by himself reaches a plane of goodness with mystical power to
heal and forgive.

Priest-confessors must investigate three mirrors. *First,* we must
look at ourselves in the mirror of our own hearts. We must be
willing to look deep into the areas we work so hard to keep hidden
from ourselves and others. *Second,* we must let others mirror how
they see us. *Third,* we must look at the truth of how God sees us
through His Word and other means of grace.

The *first mirror* is the willingness to look inside our own souls.
God creates the human soul with the ability of circumspection.
Introspection is the ability to *look inside* oneself; circumspection is
to look *around* oneself. It is the ability to see and *assess* oneself in
the context of your surroundings. It is the ability to watch yourself,
watching yourself. Imagine two mirrors ten feet apart with you in
the middle. When you look in one mirror, you see yourself in the
reflection of the other mirror. Ultimately, you can see many more
images of yourself than if you just looked at the reflection from a
single mirror.

We can look inside our soul, assess, confess, and make changes.
The Apostle Paul alludes to this circumspection mirror:

> "For what I want to do I do not do, but what I hate to
> do...Sin living in me. Good itself does not dwell in me,

that is, in my sinful nature ... for I do not do the good I want to do, but the evil I don't want to do ... this I keep doing" (Rom 7:15b-19).

Involving another person in the process, as in the confessor-*confessee* relationship, is like having two mirrors instead of one.

As a priest-confessor grows in circumspection, he can be a mirror to the *confessee*. The priest-confessor offers comfort in the face of what the *confessee* sees. The *confessee* begins to feel he is not alone. A sacred space opens when a soul looks at itself in the presence of a priest-confessor. Self-discovery touches the soul of both the speaker telling and the confessor listening. Together, the one seeing and the one listening find hope in their shared journey through life.

Few people dare exercise their capacity to look deeply within themselves. Fewer still can think outside themselves. Since the Fall of humanity, people have been more likely to blame another rather than do the work of introspection. On top of this default setting, add all the negative messages we receive in our formative years, and the look inside becomes overwhelming, depressing, even re-traumatizing. When a person looks inside himself or herself, a record of these messages resurfaces, and he or she retreats from the first mirror. The need for priest-confessors out in the *wild* is critical today to protect and connect to the *confessee*.

The inability of people to introspect creates the need for the priest-confessor. Carefully and slowly, the priest gives permission for another to unpack the overly weighted attic and the crowded, moldy basement. The confessor is patient, kind, and encouraging in this process because he or she knows how weak, heavy, and humiliating things are in his or her own life.

The *confessee*'s first look into the mirror is often the hardest. It begins to expose lost dignity. Humility, and a realistic sense of self in the priest-confessor, create safety and empower the *confessee* to take their first look. The priest-confessor has the privilege of guarding and restoring stolen dignity. Because of their own journeys, confessors in the *wild* understand others' journeys to and from the first mirror.

The *second mirror* is the one held up by others, how others see us. In 2 Samuel 11, King David has an affair with a married woman, Bathsheba. After Bathsheba becomes pregnant, David piles treachery upon treachery to cover up his sin. In the end, he has Uriah, Bathsheba's husband, sent to the front line of battle to be killed so he can marry Bathsheba. David gets away with this murderous maneuver but leaves devastating damage. The story and coverup seem contained until the prophet, Nathan, shows up on the scene and confronts David in the next chapter. Nathan forces David to look deep into the mirror of his soul and confront his own wounds and the wounds he has inflicted on others.

A priest-confessor who spends little time in the first mirror is ill-equipped to hold the second mirror up for others. Jesus argues,

> "Why do you look at the speck of sawdust in your brother's eye and pay no attention to the log beam in your own eye? How can you say, Let me take that speck out of your eye when there's a log in your own eye? You, hypocrite, remove the log first" (Matthew 7:1-4).

Jesus is *not* telling us to avoid the second mirror space with one another. He is telling us to enter this space looking deeply into our own souls first.

Why ask another human being to look into your soul and tell what they discover? Why poke the demons inside us? Only those who are willing to look at their own deeply layered sin and confess are able to hear the darkness of another's soul and not be surprised, shocked or judgmental. The priest-confessor's experience with the second mirror helps him or her care for the unsettling effect on another's soul as they look into the first.

The *third mirror* involves God showing a person how He sees him or her. Often, people have this all wrong. Many in my parish believe God is out to get them. They view Him as a judge who keeps score and pays back. Some grow up hearing moral platitudes, works-based righteousness, or fear-based preaching. This causes them to be afraid to be honest with God about their failure and sin. Many of us are simply deeply disappointed in ourselves and project our disappointment in ourselves onto God.

But a much more accurate and compelling portrayal of God as a Father is found in the Prodigal Son story in Luke 15. Maybe I see the prodigal as my alter ego. My deeper curiosity, though, is in the broken heart of the waiting father who gives his young, restless, flesh and blood his inheritance. Did the son deserve his inheritance? Of course not! Do any of us? Of course not! Yet, the father gives the son his money, and then he stands on the hill and waits for his return.

I think I deserve food, a warm bed, and a job to make money that enables travel and comfort. The prodigal son's entitlement is deeper in me than even I know. But the father's waiting creates space each day for the return of the son. I imagine the father straining to look on the horizon for any human form that might be his son returning. This is God our Father looking back in the mirror to his son and daughter. The longing look of the father also is the manner of the priest-confessor, waiting patiently on the people in his or her care.

The priest-confessor is the face and eyes of God to some, while, to others, the butt of jokes and mockery. Of course, only God Himself can forgive, heal, and save a soul. So, the priest-confessor holds these dynamics in tension, expressing the presence of God yet as a fallen human.

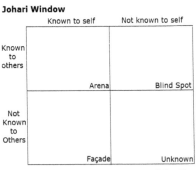

Source: Wikipedia

The Johari window illustrates the need for others to mirror things about ourselves we cannot see. Everyone experiences forces, feelings, and events which shape us in ways we are unaware and affects how we come across to others.

Five Seasons

As I look back on my time in my parish, I observe five seasons.

The *first*, I call the Clown season – "Al, are you a Clown?" Other pastors in my own tribe asked me this question. I asked this question of myself. My wife asked too! And the people in my bar asked, "Al, are you really a Pastor or did you just get your certificate in the mail?" The Clown season lasted two years as I listened to anyone's anger toward God or me. But eventually people began to tell me what hurt. After many tears, some dared to say out loud what was hidden in their souls. Through listening, hearing, holding, and interceding, faith and healing began to stir.

The *second season* in my bar sounded something like this, "Pastor Al, I don't believe all that stuff you believe, but it's okay that you believe it." Amazingly, I began to receive a wave, kind words, and even hugs when I walked into the bar. One of my dear gay friends said to me, "Look, I know you're a Billy Graham Christian-type, but, for some reason, I miss you when you're not around!" A bond of love and affection grew. We began to banter about touchy subjects – lightly at first, and more seriously later. One bar peep once said to another, "Go to hell!" Then the other turned to me asking, "Pastor Al, do you think I'm going to hell?" Eventually, this person would circle back to explore the concept at a sincere level.

The *third season* is the subject of the previous chapter and this one, "The role of the confessor." I didn't see this one coming. People needed to tell me something. Dusty, a large, professional-looking man, put his hand on my shoulder and said, "You know, God shouldn't pick on the little people." I smiled and waited before saying, "I'm sorry friend." Dusty responded, "Say a prayer for me if you can fit it in." I began to discover my purpose and place in the wild was to enter the role of the confessor.

The *fourth season* in my parish required me to become obscenely quiet. I needed to make space deep inside my own soul available to really *hear* what someone needed to say. Shifting from "Listening to Reply" to "Listening to Hear" is how I describe it now.

Somehow, I missed this class in seminary (as did every other minister I coach). The typical minister's soul is full of so much noise it has little room to hear. In my own soul, noise echoes from my parent's past words, from demons who bedevil me, from my insecurities, and from my own sins and failures. I began to let God hear me grieve these noises and voices so I could begin to hear my Master's voice in their place (Dayhoff, 2018). The fourth season required a new way of using my heart, my mind, and my faith to walk through the world listening to hear.

The *fifth season* involves partnerships – especially partnerships with non-church people to do the work of God. Are you serious, Al? Yep! For instance, my bar peeps asked me to do a book signing with the tattoo book. They think *they* wrote the tattoo book. I love it! Many invite me into their homes and places of work. In these spaces, I find heart-warming and exciting conversations. These partnerships keep developing in many sectors and in surprising ways because of the love and affection between confessor and *confessee*.

The Priest-Confessor ... How did I miss this?

"Therefore, since we have a great high priest who has ascended into heaven, Jesus the Son of God, let us hold firmly to the faith we profess. For we do not have a high priest who is unable to empathize with our weaknesses, but we have one who has been tempted in every way, just as we are—yet he did not sin. Let us then approach God's throne of grace with confidence, so that we may receive mercy and find grace to help us in our time of need." (Hebrews 4:14-16)

The Priest-Confessor ... A Personal Story

My friend, Scott Bull, is a church planter and pastor in the Atlanta area. Scott practices the role of priest-confessor in profound ways. Consider his encounter with a confessee who hesitantly opens her soul.

Shaq

"If there is a God and if He is so *good,* then why did my childhood suck so bad? Why did He let all those terrible things happen to me? No, there cannot be a God! If there is, He is a cruel person, whom I don't want anything to do with."

For months, I developed a friendship with the woman who uttered these words to me. She goes by "Shaq," stands about 6 feet 4 inches, and has a big personality also. Whenever I approach her, she shakes her head side to side, sticks her finger in my face and says, "Not tonight Pastor ... I am too stressed out, and I am not talking to you. Walk away from me."

Slowly, I learn to discern when I can playfully interact with her and when I need to walk away. I am a white, middle class pastor in a bar. She is a black woman who did not grow up middle class, and who does not believe in God. Obviously, two people like us do not typically hang out in bars together. I can only imagine what I must look like through her eyes.

On different occasions, she gives me assignments and hoops to jump through. If I do such and such, she will sit down with me, but not until then. I suspect most of Shaq's life, she has been the one hunting and chasing down people. She tests me to see if I will truly pursue friendship with her. I'm in. Patiently, I play her game.

One night, Shaq sees me, begins to turn away, and says her usual, "Not tonight Pastor! I ain't doing no interview tonight. I know I said I would next time, but I can't. Now walk away from me. I ain't playin' this time!"

As I walk away, I turn with one last plea, "Come on, Shaq, I'll buy your next drink, if you'll let me interview you."

She drops her head and smiles, saying, "What the hell!"

As we sit at a table, Shaq lays down the rules, "You're a pastor, so you're not buying my drink. You've got five minutes, white man, so go. Hurry, you're wasting both of our time."

When I ask if it felt weird to sit at the table with me, a pastor, she says, "No. Only because I have talked with other pastors before; but they all judge me. I bet, at some point tonight, you'll do the same."

I make a deal. "If at any point, you feel like I am judging you, you have my permission to punch me in the face . . . I'm gonna be knocked out if you punch me, aren't I."

"Yup," she replies smiling. She needs to be in charge, and I want her to know I know she is.

I ask about her childhood. Her story is tragic. As Shaq recounts memories of pain, loss, and heartache, she stares into the distance over my shoulders often rhetorically asking, "God, why?"

I listen, smile, frown, and cry. She looks at me long enough to catch me crying, and asks, "This is my story, not yours. Why are you crying, Pastor?"

As I compose myself, I reply, "What you went through as a child wasn't supposed to happen, and I'm so sorry it did."

She responds, "Thank you … but in a weird way, I'm thankful for what I went through. It made me who I am today."

Shaq tells me how she puts her wounds onto paper, and it lessens their power over her – somewhat. Journaling brings back some semblance of freedom for her. Yet she confesses, now looking into my eyes, "I have so much in me I don't know what to do with. Sometimes, no matter how much I write about it, I can't find healing."

With sadness, Shaq shares how she learned at a young age to be a person that takes care of others as a means of survival. "Flood your mind and heart with other people's needs and you'll forget about your own," as she finally begins to cry.

After a moment, she says, "The only problem with that ... my whole life, NO ONE has ever been there for me. NO ONE has ever loved me for who I am and me only. I only exist to give; never to receive."

Nonetheless, Shaq tells me she continues writing in hopes of soothing her soul. She is condensing her writing into chapters of a book she hopes to publish one day. She's titled it, *Surviving Through Words*. Sheepishly, Shaq asks if I might read her writing and help her edit it into a form to benefit others who need to hear a story like hers.

What began as "You have five minutes," stretches into over an hour of her telling me her story as I listen. I see the Image of God in Shaq even through her deep wounds and hopes.

At the end of our time together, I part with these words, "Shaq, I know you told me you don't believe in Jesus, and I'm fine with that. But I want you to know, I am going to talk to Jesus about you and on your behalf, regarding the hopes you shared with me. And you need to know, Jesus likes to talk with me. So, look out!"

Looking at me sternly, she replies, "You can do whatever the hell you want, Pastor."

Then she breaks into a smile, reaches across the table with her right arm and fist bumps me.

No punch in the face tonight!

How did I miss this? Confessor in the Wild.

Chapter 5: The Poet Confessor

I wonder what motivated Thomas Edison to invent the phonograph in 1877. It preceded the record player, the 8-track tape, cassettes, CD's, iPods, and now, streaming music. Perhaps one of Edison's motivations was to hear the confessions sung by the poets of each age.

Songs are a confession looking for a confessor. Listen to each generation's music, and you will hear their insightful poets sing their collective confession. You will hear common themes across the generations in their songs: lost love, money, respect, and health. Perhaps every generation needs a cacophony of singers to make their confession again, so it won't be lost. Every age tells its unique confession; ours is an age of nuclear weapons, race riots, HIV, Vietnam war, abortion, rising divorce rates, gender confusion, #metoo, the Rustbelt, cancer, and the Covid-19 pandemic. Could it be that the music we love might contain the sound and words of our own confession?

Songwriters, aware of most simple pleasures and deepest sorrows, put their pain into poetic verse, moving the soul and body to unite in dance. When musicians play together and the room dances in response, band, and audience experience something magically soulish, almost sacred. The animating message inside the music and movement is the poet speaking the confession.

From my generation's musical era, the Sixties, I hear these confessions.

Love is a Battlefield, Pat Benatar

A world without heroes is like a world without
sun, you lookup to anyone, Kiss

If I leave here tomorrow, would you still
remember me? Lynyrd Skynyrd

Hard Day's Night, The Beatles

I was born with a plastic spoon in my mouth,
The Who

Where do I go now that I've gone too far,
Golden Earring.

When a person has no pastor, priest, or confessor, to whom does one go to unburden the soul? Remember, there are secrets, hidden hurts, and violations of dignity festering inside the soul and waiting for a confessor. Why do we listen to songs over and over? Why are songs so easy to memorize? Why do we hum the tune when showering or driving? It may be because a song is a confession looking for a confessor. Our poets are singing the hurts our souls are desperate to reveal.

"Is There More," Drake

Good hearted people are takin' it to extremes
Leavin' me in limbo to question what I

---

believe
Leavin' me to ask what's their motive
and makin' peace

Leavin' me to not trust anybody I meet

Leavin' me to ask is there anybody like me?

Original Poetry and the First Blues Singer

When the earth is formless and void and the Spirit of God hovers, God speaks creation into existence. God speaks mankind into existence, in His image, from the dust of the ground. Man hears God's voice for the first time. He reflects his Creator by speaking names for all the animals. As God sees all his creation and hears its sounds He declares and repeats, it is all GOOD!

Initially, the man is alone to work and care for God's garden. There is no one like him to whom he may talk and listen. So, God causes a deep sleep to fall over man and fashions a partner who also can also speak, create, and bring beauty into the world. In poetic awe, the man says she is "Bone of my bone, and flesh of my flesh," and calls her "woman." They are naked, and feel no shame, and God walks with them in the garden. Together, God, man, and woman hear each other and all the sounds in creation.

God speaks to the man and warns him that if he eats from the tree of the knowledge of good and evil, he will die. God commissions the woman and man to exercise dominion over creation and care for the garden. One of their responsibilities is to steward sound – to order it into words, sentences, stories, poetry, and song.

But evil emerges in the garden in the form of a talking serpent. The serpent tempts the woman, "You could be like God if you eat of the tree of the knowledge of good and evil" (Genesis 3:5). And when the woman and man eat of the forbidden tree, immediately, shame engulfs them. Their souls are forever marked with guilt and shame.

Adam and Eve fall from the glory for which they are made. They use their voices to blame, perhaps the first confession. God uses his voice to announce the consequences of their disobedience. Ultimately, God speaks words driving them from paradise into a cold world now filled with sounds of tears, heartbreak, and suffering.

In a manner of speaking, the Fall created the first Blues singer. A Blues singer channels the sounds of a fallen world. They cry about things not being how it should and the reality it cannot be restored. Millennia before the genre of Blues, David began his Psalm 22, "My God, my God, why have you forsaken me." On the Cross, Jesus feels cast from the Garden of God's care and joins David in his cry of loneliness and despair. Forsaken!

"Why have you forsaken me?" is the heart's cry to God when evil and heartache dominate, and God seems silent and inactive. Another way the Bible and the Blues ask the question is, "How long, O Lord?" (Psalm 13:1)

Every Blues singer knows the tune of the soul and puts it in verse, a confession to the ears of God. Whatever your contemporary musical style – Jazz, Pop, Soul, Rhythm and Blues, Rap, Country, Heavy Metal, Big Band, Rockabilly, and even Gospel – each collects the confessions of the soul and sings them to all who will hear. Great songs are confessions of the soul, resonating deeply within us. Thoughts put to words. Words put to music. A musician sings the confession.

"Creep," Radiohead

I don't care if it hurts.

I want to have control.

I want a perfect body;

I want a perfect soul.

I want you to notice,

When I'm not around.

You're so "very" special.

I wish I was special.

But I'm a creep

I'm a weirdo

What the hell am I doing here?

I don't belong here...

The Psalms as Confessions

Why do David's Psalms both confuse and draw us in? Many of David's lyrics cannot be used in the average contemporary Protestant church service because they are not clean enough, not upbeat enough, and are potentially confusing. Indeed, some Psalms should be saved for private reading and introspection. People often categorize different psalms as adoration, contrition, thanksgiving, and supplication. Yet all, in some manner, are confessions of the heart. Confession is not just admitting where we have gone wrong. Confessions are the soul's cry for meaning, hope, and healing. They are a cry and longing for God, as a soul enters the process of conversion.

> Look and see, there is no one at my right hand; no one is concerned for me. I have no refuge; no one cares for my life. I cry to you, Lord; I say,

> "You are my refuge, my portion in the land of the living. Listen to my cry, for I am in desperate need; rescue me from those who pursue me, for they are too strong for me. Set me free from my prison, that I may praise your name. Then the righteous will gather about me because of your goodness to me" (Psalm 142).

> "Be merciful to me, O LORD, for I am in distress; My life is consumed by anguish and my years by groaning; my strength fails because of my affliction, and my bones grow weak. Because of all my enemies, I am the utter contempt of my neighbors; I am a dread to my friends – those who see me on the street flee from me. I am forgotten by them as though I were dead; I have become like broken pottery. For I hear the slander of many; there is terror on every side; they conspire against me and plot to take my life. But I trust in you, O LORD; I say, "You are my God." My times are in your hands; deliver me from my enemies and from those who pursue me. Let your face shine on your servant; save me in your unfailing love" (Psalm 31).

> "Lord, do not rebuke me in your anger or discipline me in your wrath. Have mercy on me, Lord, for I am faint; heal me, Lord, for my bones are in agony. My soul is in deep

anguish. How long, Lord, how long? Turn, Lord, and deliver me; save me because of your unfailing love. Among the dead no one proclaims your name. Who praises you from the grave? I am worn out from my groaning" (Psalm 6).

The Psalms and other portions of the Old Testament are a collection of the soul's confession to others and to God.

Are the greatest songs tied to the deepest confessions of the soul?

The Blues as Confession

Jimmy Cole is a dear friend, singer, songwriter, and musician. Jimmy is part of Blue Church, the name of our church in the bar, and a spiritual leader in the Blues music community in the Washington, DC area. When I hear Jimmy sing, my soul shakes. This vibration of my soul happens because his life experience and voice transport me to a space where confession for me is safe.

Jimmy knows the mystical interplay between the band and the dancers. Dancers put bodily form to the words and music. They call out to each other, and the dance becomes part of the Confession. Lyrics bring out the pain, loss, or hard times "a-comin'," and they inspire a certain choreography unique to each dancer. Perhaps people dance to the Blues because pain in the soul yearns to be confessed bodily.

When Jimmy sings blues, I suspect he intuitively pivots off Jesus' desperate words on the Cross to His Father, "Why have you forsaken me?" The body moves in response to "forsaken," sometimes writhing, sometimes running, sometimes isolating from relationship, or sometimes using alcohol as a partner. The soul dances, and our bodies move to express our souls.

Jimmy speaks the confessions written by our poets, our songwriters looking for someone to listen, someone to hear. When he plays his guitar, you see Jimmy embodying these confessions. To borrow a phrase from The Eagles, "Some dance to remember; some dance to forget" (Look for *Why We Dance*, to be released in 2021).

Jimmy is made to be a confessor – someone who listens, hears, holds, and watches faith and healing stir. Yet, instead of God calling him into the priesthood, God has called him to be a confessor on stage, behind a microphone, in honky-tonks, in Blues bars, late at night for fifty-five-plus years. In my opinion, it's an equally legitimate calling.

When Jimmy begins to unwind all his memories of people, bands, lyrics, and gigs into words, they come fast and hard. He is a consummate storyteller. It's what he does. When I experience Jimmy's intensity, I wonder if his urgency is fueled by being afraid, he will forget the stories. I wonder whether he is worried others will not remember when a certain blues singer channeled the hidden pain of those on the dance floor or hidden in a corner booth.

I ask Jimmy about his "call." He says, "I was born this way."

When I push for more, he replies, "I'm a *Songster*."

I'm a Songster

"What's that?" I ask.

"You play whatever you can play, what moves people, what moves you as an artist. I travel late at night over long distances because I must. It's what I do. I don't play music and then work. I work so I can play music. So much of the music, maybe all of it, comes out of the church. Listen to the lyrics. You will hear the song talking to God – what hurts, what's lost, the love of simple things. Where there is a thought, a word, or a sound, we are talking to God, making a confession," Jimmy answers.

I'm glad I pushed him for more! Then, I take a different approach, "What's your favorite song you have written?"

"I haven't written it yet, Al. I'm a Songster. It doesn't matter if I write it or not. My job is to match the song with the band and the audience – and do it again, the next night!"

The Songster's on a roll now!

"Al, my devotion to music caused me problems, but I did the best I could. But you know what? I sense the spirit of God is often in the room, often speaking and creating an experience many will remember for years to come and reflect on when they are old. Each generation must say its peace to God, get it out, tell what's on their heart or hidden in their subconscious. Some let music do it for them.

"Al, sometimes you will see people grooving to the music or mouthing the words. They are part of the message, the speaking to God or whoever there is to listen. My confessor is the Spirit of God. He shows up in the bar, in the moment when a man is still on a stool at the counter rethinking his life. We sound out that man's "wailing to God." The stereotype of people who come to the honky-tonk or Blues bar being "down and out" is not true. I believe people in a bar have a lot to hear and give back to God.

"I'm a Songster. I play songs people seem to need. Maybe the song puts into words, sound and poetry, what people have been trying to say to God. The band is not always sure where the song will take us. But often the dancers respond, telling us with their moves, 'Please do it again.' Often people come up to me and bare their souls. Over the years, I've learned to just listen, because that's what they need and want. It's just what I do, Al.

"God was up to something special when we first met in Sully's Blues Bar in Chantilly, Virginia seven years ago. You were on a very special journey from your brick-and-mortar church to your Blue Church. I got to be part of the journey. I remember you saying, "That song moved me tonight." Little did I know what God was up to. The Spirit can go in any juke-joint and feel right at home – always ready to listen or put things into words and songs. Many nights, Al, the bar was in the Book of Lamentations, and the band was singing the lyrics. Blues is God's music. Maybe the Spirit is a Songster of the soul?"

I asked Jimmy to be part of this book because, well, he is way cooler than I am. Jimmy's demeanor and way of being tells a story of a long life in interesting places – where, late at night, people "say it" to the Songster in the bar, in the dance and through the band. He's been far and wide, heard a lot, lost, and regained a lot. He is way more thankful than regretful but has regrets just the same. God put Jimmy in the very bar I was hiding in some seven years ago. Jimmy, the Songster, helped me find a new gig. I was walking on Christian carpet, doing Christian handshakes, drinking Christian coffee yet SO needed the *wild* – the place where men and women come to tell what's on their soul.

Jimmy looks older now. His eyes say much. Each line on his face tells a story, of a feeling, a hard night on the road, lost loves, and bands that broke up. With a few hours of sleep, though, he's ready for the next gig. Tired from loading speakers, soundboards, and drums in his truck, Jimmy still responds to his call to speak the confessions of a songwriter, a generation, and his own soul. Jimmy claims he will never be too old to play.

I thank God for Jimmy Cole, my friend who listens to the Spirit who led Him to Sully's Blues Bar. I was a wanderer in the audience, trying so hard to hide and yet still somehow find my next assignment in God's Kingdom. Jimmy's songs spoke *my* confessions. It's been the greatest journey!

Oh, and if you wait around and meet Jimmy, he will listen to you – your own confessions reaching out to a confessor. But if you can't make it to out to hear him in person, you can listen to his confessions at www.Jimmycolemusic.com. Who knows? You might find your own confessions in his songs like I do.

"My God, my God, why have you forsaken me? Why are you so far from saving me, so far from my cries of anguish? My God, I cry out by day, but you do not answer by night, but I find no rest" (Psalm 22:1-2).

Final Thoughts

To understand the music of each generation requires listening to hear – hearing the story behind the words, the life behind the poet, the connection each generation makes with songs they can't play enough. The longevity of a song, songwriter, or singer may speak more of the depth and resonation of the confession encapsulated in the song. One such singer-poet, James Taylor, begins his song "Secret o' Life" with the line, "The secret of life is enjoying the passage of time."

The Poet Confessor ... How did I miss this?

Chapter 6: Animal Confessors

Why do we love to go to the beach? Lavish forests? Majestic mountains? Flowing rivers? Disney's animal park?

In our body and soul, we seek the Garden of Eden – whether we realize it or not.

Walking along the beach in Indonesia, I experience God's response to his creation: "It is good" (Genesis 1:10) in all my senses. I think, "If the Garden of Eden looked like this, I understand why God looked at what His words formed and declared, 'It is good!'"

A woman, with a puppy nipping at her heels, approaches. I can't help but smile and admire the puppy. The woman responds in a German accent, "I found her on a trash heap, she says of the puppy. I think someone threw her away. But I contacted an agency for the paperwork to take her back to Germany. They gave her a computer chip, and I gave her a name. So, she's official now."

I reply, "How lucky the puppy is to have found you!"

"We found each other!" she exclaims.

A dog whisperer called to rescue this puppy? I wonder, "Does God anoint some with the skill to see, hear, and protect animals? Do animals need a confessor? Someone who hears their "voice?" Maybe they do.

When my friends, Gabriel and Susie, anticipated the birth of their first child, they read all the consumer reviews before buying the perfect crib. When baby Chloe was born, they placed her in the crib, along with a gift from Grandma – a mobile playing "twinkle, twinkle little star." It was complete with a sun, moon, and various animals dangling above.

Interestingly, whether by mobiles or stuffed animals, we introduce our newborns to the creation of animals. Before words, we teach them the sounds animals make. Why? The blessing upon Creation, the Creation Mandate, from Genesis! Perhaps we incubate animal confessors from birth.

> When I consider your heavens, the work of your fingers,
> the moon and the stars, which you have set in place,
> what is mankind that you are mindful of him,
> human beings that you care for them?
> You have made them a little lower than the angels
> and crowned them with glory and honor.
> You made them rulers over the works of your hands;
> you put everything under their feet:
> all flocks and herds, and the animals of the wild,
> the birds in the sky, and the fish in the sea,
> all that swim the paths
> of the seas (Psalm 8:3-7).

An Animal Confessor

My wife Deb and I love the delicious delight of setting up our camp kitchen and canopied living room at Assateague Island Beach in Maryland. One morning, I awakened with desire for someone to make me an extra hot, flat, white latte in a ceramic mug and call my name. Sitting at an outside table at a Starbucks in Ocean City, Maryland, I tie my ninety-eight-pound chocolate Labrador, Klee, to my chair. Klee gets a venti whipped cream, his whole body wagging in sheer delight!

A woman walks by with four coffees, a large purse, a sunburn, and a "who cares?" hairdo, trying to not spill the specialty coffees. Then she sees Klee and stops.

"Aren't you the most handsome boy I've ever seen?" she says.

Klee's big square head begins to sniff the air. I want to reply for him, "Well, thank you very much!" But something stops me from hijacking the moment and making myself the one seen and heard. She begins to talk to Klee.

"I've missed you. It's been three years since you passed. Your bed is still in the corner, but I've recently given away your toys."

I realize a sacred moment is unfolding. Something deep inside this woman is getting released. I keep silent. She blinks back tears.

"We are all doing okay. But we haven't been able to get another dog yet. What's your name?"

Now I answer for him, "His name is Klee," while she maintains eye contact with my dog.

"Klee, I hope you play in the waves and live for many years." Somehow, she bends down while still balancing the coffees and herself to pat Klee gently. Slowly she whispers, "I love you."

And she is gone.

What is that? How does an ordinary Starbucks moment turn into real level pain from the soul getting released with tears? Maybe it was Klee's mile long tongue licking the bottom of the whipped cream cup. Perhaps his eyes ignited her confession. Klee became her confessor.

Animals in God's Story

God's unfolding story in the Scriptures begins with God speaking the Garden into existence. It is a paradise of unimaginable beauty, variety, and exploration. God makes man from the dust of the earth and breathes life into him, so he becomes a living being. God, then, charges mankind to help flourish all spheres of creation, including animal life. Adam is given the responsibility of speaking each animal's name into existence. God conveys to Adam that even the animals have a special role in God's creation.

> Now out of the ground the Lord God had formed every beast of the field and every bird of the heavens and brought them to the man to see what he would call them. And whatever the man called every living creature, that was its name. The man gave names to all livestock and to the birds of the heavens and to every beast of the field (Genesis 2:19-20).

Talk about a great first job. Naming the animals? Sign me up! From the beginning, God calls man to relate, speak, perhaps even, listen to the animals.

As a result of Adam and Eve's fall from glory in Eden, mankind is cast from the Garden. All of creation, including the earth and animals, pay a price for man's sin. The animal kingdom turns carnivorous, and all of nature experiences haunting pain and groaning. Creation itself begins to long for restoration. Though fallen, creation still retains the capacity for wonder and magnificence. Each human soul, reflecting God's image, seeks to re-find this paradise and relationship with God amid struggle and pain.

> By the sweat of your brow, you will eat your food until you return to the ground, since from it you were taken; for dust you are and to dust you will return. Adam named his wife Eve because she would become the mother of all the living. The Lord God made garments of skin for Adam and his wife and clothed them (Genesis 3:19-20).

When God judges and destroys the earth because of mankind's downward spiral of sin, God calls Noah to rescue the animals. Noah enters the ark with every animal according to its kind in pairs. When Noah leaves the ark, he offers animals and birds on an altar as burnt offerings pleasing God. Yet, Noah also leads all living creatures out into creation so they may all be fruitful and multiply and fill the earth.

After Noah's rescue, offering, and renewal of the covenant of Creation, God makes a big promise to Abraham to make him the father of many peoples in a land God will provide. God initiates this covenant with Abraham by animal sacrifices.

[God] also said to him, "I am the LORD, who brought you out of Ur of the Chaldeans to give you this land to take possession of it. But Abram said, "Sovereign LORD, how can I know that I will gain possession of it?" So, the LORD said to him, "Bring me a heifer, a goat and a ram, each three years old, along with a dove and a young pigeon." Abram brought all these to him, cut them in two and arranged the halves opposite each other; the birds, however, he did not cut in half. Then birds of prey came down on the carcasses, but Abram drove them away (Genesis 15:7-11).

Animals split in two was a common covenant-making ceremony of Abraham's time in which both parties stand in between the divided animals. In this instance, God makes Abraham fall into a deep sleep, and God shows up alone in the midst of the animal sacrifice to show He alone can keep this covenant promise.

Animals Used for our Sins

Animals pay the price for the Fall though humans are the ones who sinned. God requires offerings of animal life as a substitute payment for man's sin.

> Then to the sons of Israel you shall speak, saying, "Take a male goat for a sin offering, and a calf and a lamb, both one year old, without defect, for a burnt offering" (Leviticus 9:3).

> Then on the eighth day he shall bring two turtledoves or two young pigeons to the priest, to the doorway of the tent of meeting. The priest shall offer one for a sin offering and the other for a burnt offering and make atonement for him

concerning his sin because of the dead person. And that same day he shall consecrate his head. He shall present his offering to the LORD: one male lamb a year old without defect for a burnt offering and one ewe-lamb a year old without defect for a sin offering and one ram without defect for a peace offering (Numbers 6:10-11,14).

Not only are animal life and human life intertwined in creation and a fallen creation but also in God's covenant promise and atonement for sin.

Consider Job's perspective on what man can learn from animals.

But ask the beasts, and they will teach you; the birds of the heavens, and they will tell you; or the bushes of the earth, and they will teach you; and the fish of the sea will declare to you. Who among all these does not know that the hand of the Lord has done this? In his hand is the life of every living thing and the breath of all mankind (Job 12:7-10).

Creation knows things about God the human mind resists.

Consider God and man's relationship to animals from poetic literature in the Scriptures.

I know every bird in the heights; whatever moves in the wild is mine (Psalm 50:11).

The righteous care for the needs of their animals, but the kindest acts of the wicked are cruel (Proverbs 12:10).

Are not two sparrows sold for a penny? Yet not one of them will fall to the ground outside your Father's care (Matthew 10:29).

God knows every animal! His righteous ones care for animals. Isaiah prophesies restoration between animal life and people.

> The wolf will live with the lamb, the leopard will lie down with the goat, the calf and the lion and the yearling together; and a little child will lead them. The cow will feed with the bear, their young will lie down together, and the lion will eat straw like the ox. The infant will play near the cobra's den, and the young child will put its hand into the viper's nest. They will neither harm nor destroy on all my holy mountain, for the earth will be filled with the knowledge of the Lord as the waters cover the sea (Isaiah 11:6-9).

No more survival of the fittest in animal life! No more fear of snakes for children and their parents! The knowledge of the Lord will fill all of creation and heal from all harm.

Before a restored earth is possible, the Creator, Jesus Christ, comes as the ultimate substitute payment in the form of a helpless babe – surrounded by creation and animals.

> The time came for the baby to be born, and she gave birth to her firstborn, a son. She wrapped him in cloths and placed him in a manger, because there was no guest room available for them. And there were shepherds living out in the fields nearby, keeping watch over their flocks at night. An angel of the Lord appeared to them, and the glory of the Lord shone around them, and they were terrified. But the angel said to them, "Do not be afraid. I bring you good

news that will cause great joy for all the people. Today in the town of David a Savior has been born to you; he is the Messiah, the Lord. This will be a sign to you: You will find a baby wrapped in cloths and lying in a manger (Luke 2:6-12).

The infant Jesus, lying in a feeding trough, announced to shepherds out in the fields, showing God's incarnation at the intersection of men and animals once again.

The ending of Jesus's first advent begins at this same point of intersection.

This took place to fulfill what was spoken through the prophet: "Say to Daughter Zion, 'See, your king comes to you gentle and riding on a donkey, and on a colt, the foal of a donkey.'" The disciples went and did as Jesus had instructed them. ⁷ They brought the donkey and the colt and placed their cloaks on them for Jesus to sit on (Matthew 21:5-7).

In place of relying on animal offerings to atone for mankind's sin, Jesus Christ, Himself, in His death on the cross becomes the ultimate and final offering so animals would no longer pay the price for man's sin.

For the bodies of those animals whose blood is brought into the holy place by the high priest as an offering for sin, are burned outside the camp. Therefore, Jesus also suffered outside the gate that He might sanctify the people through His own blood (Hebrews 13:11-12).

At the beginning of Jesus's second advent, He comes riding an animal more battle-ready than a donkey.

I saw heaven standing open and there before me was a white horse, whose rider is called Faithful and True (Revelation 19:11).

So, Christ comes as the way of deliverance and salvation for a cursed creation. "Whosoever shall call upon the name of the Lord shall be saved." Ultimately, a new heaven and new earth full of God's splendor will be in store as creation gets restored to its fullest wonder and magnificence.

St. Francis

A well-known figure from church history is St. Francis of Assisi. Francis was born in Italy in 1182. Growing up in a wealthy but abusive home, Francis eventually renounces his father and forsakes his inheritance. Sainted for his devotion to Christ and the establishing of the Franciscan Order, Francis eventually becomes more known for his love for animals.

Though not ordained by the church, Francis begins to serve at the chapel, St. Mary of the Angels, where he takes care of lepers near Assisi. He devotes himself to a life of poverty. He exchanges his fine clothes for a coarse woolen tunic with a knotted rope serving as his belt, as worn by the poorest Umbrian peasants. He travels the countryside to call people to penance, brotherly love, and peace. As he travels and ministers, Francis blesses and cares for animals.

Stories abound of Francis's love and sometimes mystical relationship with animals. On one occasion he happens upon a merchant carrying two small lambs to market. Moved by the plaintive bleating of the lambs, he asks the peasant, "Why do you torment my brothers the lambs?" When he learns the man intends to sell them for slaughter, he declares, "That will not happen!" and buys them from the man. At Portiuncula for many years, he has a tame lamb which follows him everywhere, even into the church, where its bleating mingles with the chants of the brethren.

Perhaps the most famous story is of him interceding on behalf of a local village with a wolf that was terrorizing the inhabitants. Confronting the animal, the wolf becomes docile and repentant. Francis brings the wolf into the town where, miraculously, the wolf remains with and is cared for by the townspeople.

St. Francis's protection and blessing of animals is a demonstration of the Creation Mandate upon all mankind. Folklore develops about St. Francis walking and talking with animals. His story reflects God's heart for animal life. Today, many St. Francis statues portray him holding a bird. In his honor, the Church introduced a liturgy for "The Blessings of the Animals," usually held on the Sunday closest to his feast day of October 4. Perhaps these responses to Francis fill people's imagination, intuition, a God-given heart for the value of animals (Francis, 2001).

Jacques-Yves Cousteau

Yes, Jacques-Yves Cousteau. Indulge me before you judge me!

Each generation seems to have a unique protector and confessor for animals – whether a part of Christ's church or not. The great Jacques-Yves Cousteau, born in 1910, ends his aviation career in the French Navy after an auto accident. Yet Jacques continues in the Navy on the seas. Cousteau's diving expeditions for select missions during World War II allow him to discover a world in the ocean. His interest in the mysterious sea grows into a life passion and study. After leaving the French Navy, he continues diving, exploration, and research in his vessel *Calypso* (Cousteau, 2002).

Cousteau's book, *The Silent World: A Story of Undersea Discovery and Adventure*, published in 1953, offers the following observations.

> The sea, once it casts its spell, holds one in its net of wonder forever.

> For most of history, man has had to fight nature to survive; in this century he is beginning to realize that, in order to survive, he must protect it.

> The future is in the hands of those who explore... and from all the beauty they discover while crossing perpetually receding frontiers, they develop for nature and for humankind an infinite love. The best way to observe a fish is to become a fish! When we return wild animals to nature, we merely return them to what is already theirs. For men cannot give wild animals freedom, they can only take it away (Cousteau, 1953).

Jacques-Yves Cousteau–a Confessor of the Sea.

Valerie Jane Goodall

Another famous historical figure expresses God's image in love for animals. As a child in London in the 1930's, Valerie Jane Goodall received a stuffed chimpanzee from her father. The chimpanzee, named Jubilee, incubates in Jane an animal confessor imagination. She prefers Jubilee to her dolls!

As an adult in 1957, Jane visits a preserve in Kenya at a time when Louis Leaky, the famous archaeologist and paleontologist needs help studying real chimpanzees. Leakey hires Jane and sends her to Gombe Stream National Park where her passion for the chimpanzee intensifies. Seeing her raw talent, Leaky recommends Goodall to the University of Cambridge to work on a PhD in Ethology. Remarkably, Jane becomes only the eighth person in Cambridge history without an undergraduate degree to enter a PhD program. Parallel to her academic study, Jane lives among the chimpanzees in Gombe Stream Park.

As Jane observes the chimpanzees, she names each animal rather assigning them customary numbers. Her presence among these creatures results in her being accepted into a chimpanzee family for two years, as their lowest caste member. She observes chimpanzees making tools for gathering food. Jane discerns individual personalities and affections as she observes their interaction. These primates hug, kiss, and tickle each other. Families of chimpanzees remain bonded throughout their lives. Yet she also she observes factions between families growing into battles and murder (Goodall, 2002).

In 2010, when asked if she believes in God, Jane Goodall replied,

> I don't have any idea of who or what God is. But I do believe in some great spiritual power. I feel it particularly when I'm out in nature. It's just something that's bigger and stronger than what I am or what anybody is. I feel it. And it's enough for me.

Jane Goodall spent her life enthralled with this profound primate. The wonders of the animal world are for all to enjoy. But some are called to be their confessor – a soul hearing the voice of the animals and speaking on their behalf.

David Attenborough

Sir David Attenborough's name may not be as familiar as his voice. He is the narrator of BBC's *Natural History* documentary series. Spending his childhood collecting stones, fossils and other natural specimens, young David's bedroom doubled as his own museum!

In 1965, Attenborough filmed and narrated a feature on elephants in Tanzania. In 1969, he featured wildlife in Bali, Indonesia. In 1971, he filmed a previously unknown tribe in New Guinea. His filmmaking reached new heights in the *Life on Earth* series produced in 1979. Attenborough's unique skill in making animals into film stars wins respect from scientists and politicians alike as the BBC's *Natural History* becomes famous. His cinematography takes viewers from continent to continent within just one sentence of narration.

Attenborough's climactic work, *The Living Planet*, provides a window into the lives of plants, birds, and mammals. Thirty-two honorary degrees recognize his seventy years of documentaries. His lifetime exploration, protection, and advocacy for ecology on our planet are his legacy. At this writing, he continues in this calling at the age of 93!

Consider Attenborough's sentiment in his own words:

> I am intoxicated by animals. Ever since we arrived on this planet as a species, we've cut it down, dug it up, burnt it and poisoned it. Today we're doing so on a greater scale than ever. I can't pretend that I got involved with filming the natural world fifty years ago because I had some great banner to carry about conservation—not at all, I always had a huge pleasure in just watching the natural world and

seeing what happens. It seems to me that the natural world is the greatest source of excitement, the greatest source of visual beauty, the greatest source of intellectual interest. It is the greatest source of so much in life that makes life worth living (Attenborough, 2002).

The whole of life is coming to terms with yourself and the natural world. Why are you here? How do you fit in? What's it all about?

Sir David Attenborough's voice speaks for the earth and its animal inhabitants. A True confessor for the Animals in our time.

Steve Irwin

In our recent television era, Steve Irwin popularized the animal world to new levels. Irwin, born in 1962 in Melbourne, Australia to a herpetologist (his father) and a wildlife rehabilitator (his mother), practically grows up in a small reptile park in Queensland. At age six, Steve receives a twelve-foot scrub python for his birthday. His dad coaches him how to handle and wrestle crocodiles. As a young adult Steve joins crocodile rescue and relocation efforts.

Steve Irwin gained worldwide fame as "The Crocodile Hunter" in wildlife documentaries. Steve's love and passion for animals captures faithful followers and inspires millions to care for animals all over our planet. Eventually, he declares himself a "wildlife warrior" and devotes his own money to save endangered species. While snorkeling in Port Douglas, Queensland, a stingray sends a barb through Irwin's heart, causing him to bleed to death. Millions mourn. Quite appropriately, his family buries him at the Australian Zoo.

Lines from Crocodile Hunter reflect Irwin's legacy.

> I have no fear of losing my life. If I have to save a koala, a crocodile, a kangaroo, or a snake, mate – I will save it!

> Crikey means gee whiz, wow!

> It's up to us to save the animals. (Irwin, 2003)

Steve Irwin – a Confessor and Protector for the animals.

Final Thoughts

We find ourselves in an age of "Great Extinction." We are losing the animal kingdom at an alarming rate due to pollution, poaching, and destroyed habitats. The accumulation of plastics in the deepest parts of our oceans threatens sea life. Creation is groaning under the weight of mankind's sin. Who will fulfill the Creation Mandate to be creation's confessor and Protector?

Will heaven be full of animals? Yes! Will God re-create your pet or new ones? Maybe, yes! Will you and I experience deepened gratitude for animals–especially animals whose blood served as payment for man's sin until Christ's sacrifice? Oh, yes!

I know crazy animal people. Those who think their dogs have secret lives, horses have healing powers, birds impart the wonder of freedom, and dolphins have a sense of humor. My natural inclination is to dismiss such people as a bit kooky. But I have discovered something. People with an unstoppable love of animals, who often project on them human abilities, who can hear their "voices," sense their needs, protect them, and are drawn to any animal they see. These people are very close to exhibiting the heart of God.

These animal confessors have a remarkable energy enabling them to hear and see animals. God uses His image bearers to care for animal life whether Christ followers or not. Perhaps the church needs to become more aware of this aspect of mankind's stewardship. The church in the wild will find image bearers who take this more seriously than many who profess faith in the Creator, our Lord Jesus Christ.

In the Garden, in a sense, animals and humans related to each other as confessors. To understand a confessor's role in the *wild*, we may learn from those who reflect God's heart for animals and speak for them.

The Animal Confessor … How did I miss this?

Chapter 7: The Confessor, Mister Rogers

In a 2019 interview, Tom Hanks admits his initial dislike of the TV show, *Mister Rogers' Neighborhood* (1968-2001). In preparation for portraying Rogers in the dramatic recreation *A Beautiful Day In The Neighborhood*, Hanks watches hours and hours of footage of the show. It was only then he realizes, "This show is not for me! *Mister Rogers was explaining to confused beings how the world works because they actually had no impression of how it works.*"

In an age of declining civility, the story of Mister Rogers is being revisited. Even before the Hanks film, the documentary, *Won't You Be My Neighbor?* highlights Fred Rogers behind the scenes. Perhaps this is the case because we need Mister Rogers' gentleness and kindness now more than ever. In our ever-changing world, we need someone to help us process how the world works.

Fred Rogers' Childhood

Fred Rogers grew up in Latrobe, a small manufacturing town near Pittsburgh where he was bullied and nicknamed, "Fat Freddy." Often sick, he played alone, creating make-believe stories with puppets, and expressing his emotion on the piano. Sensing his childhood struggle, his grandfather would frequently say, "Freddy, I love you just the way you are. You are special. There is no one in the world quite like you, and people can like you just the way you are. You know how? By just you, being you." This message of acceptance shaped Fred Rogers' life. It became the core message he shared with each person he met.

As a freshman in high school, Fred volunteered to take homework to an injured star athlete in the hospital and a friendship formed. When the fellow student returned to school, Rogers had someone to stick up for him. Consequently, Fred began to experience his grandfather's prophetic words. Rogers became editor of the yearbook, president of the student council, and was voted "Most Likely to Succeed." He graduated as salutatorian of his class (Rogers, 2002).

In a childhood filled with rejection, followed by healing acceptance, a confessor formed. As Freddy grew up to become Mister Rogers, he never forgot what it was like to be a small child and bullied. Mister Rogers became a confessor for children.

"For you created my inmost being; you knit me together in my mother's womb. I praise you because I am fearfully and wonderfully made" (Psalm 139:13-14).

Education of a Childhood Confessor

Fred graduated from college in 1951 with a degree in music. He had planned to go to seminary and become an ordained minister. However, after watching children's programming on the new technology of television, Rogers grew concerned for the dignity of children. Seeing through the consumerism and cheap laughs of throwing pies in people's faces, Rogers moved to New York City to work in television at NBC Studios, hoping to use this new medium to promote the emotional development of children. Rogers eventually pursued a Master of Divinity degree and in 1963 was ordained as a presbyterian minister.

Rogers was a student of child psychologist Dr. Margaret McFarland, who told him, when he started *Mister Rogers' Neighborhood,* "Fred, I think to the child, that the television show between you and the child is a real relationship," as related in the documentary. Rogers viewed this space between the camera and the viewer as "holy ground."

A Rogers biographer, Shea Tuttle, explains,

> Fred's unique insight into children was his ability to stay connected to his own childhood. Fred knew intimately the current fear mixed with elation that runs through so much of childhood, the electricity of the outside world that makes the return home so very sweet. And so, he worked hard, every day of his television career, every time he looked into the camera's lens, to offer something of that home to the children [and adults] that watched. In the space between his gaze and the gaze of each child watching, he created an intimate world of safety and calm (Tuttle, p. 13).

Rogers wanted children to know feelings are mentionable and manageable.

> When we people can understand our feelings and talk about them, we are free to be who we like being ... Children have very deep feelings, just as their parents do; just like everybody does. Our striving to understand those feelings and to better respond to them is what I feel is a most

important task in our world" (*Won't You Be My Neighbor?* 2018).

Rogers believed the most important thing about learning is accepting and expecting mistakes in order to respond to the disappointments they bring.

Then people brought little children to Jesus for him to place his hands on them and pray for them. But the disciples rebuked them. Jesus said, "Let the little children come to me, and do not hinder them, for the kingdom of heaven belongs to such as these" (Matthew 19:13-14).

Theology of a Childhood Confessor

Mister Rogers affirms the Image of God in children. At the end of his show he frequently says,

> It gives me a good feeling to think that I will be with you again tomorrow. You are special. There's no one in the world quite like you. Everyone can like you exactly the way you are; and you know how, don't you? By just you, being you.

Through his songs, Rogers affirms God's image by singing, "I like you exactly as you are, exactly and precisely. I think you turned out nicely and I like you as you are." Though some criticize him as having nurtured a narcissistic, self-entitled generation, Rogers was not promoting self-entitlement but the inherent dignity and worth of image-bearers.

Tuttle quotes Rogers as saying, "It's very theological, what we do." Reflecting further, Tuttle writes,

In truth, Fred could have said that about pretty much any aspect of his life. He was a religious person through and through, extraordinarily thoughtful and intentional, and his faith was constantly present to him ... [he said], "Anything that's a part of me becomes a part of the program. My relationship with God, which I feel is very comfortable and healthy, cannot ever be disassociated from who I am on the program, even though I don't deal in overt theological terms. Our dialogue with children constantly includes acceptance of someone exactly as she or he is at the moment. I feel that's how God operates. Jesus tells us in no uncertain terms that I like you as you are and let's grow together from there" (Tuttle, p. 4).

Rogers credits Jesus as his motivation: "When I say what we do is theological, I'm referring to the Incarnation. The Incarnation means man is not isolated. There is Someone who cares and understands." (Rogers, 25). Tuttle amplifies Rogers' incarnational approach:

Mister Rogers's responses to his viewer's fears were patient, serious, and thorough. He didn't ask kids to stop being afraid – though sometimes careful explanations did alleviate fear – or to stop crying. (It angered Fred to hear adults tell children not to cry, even when adults were trying to offer comfort.) Instead, he offered a kind of incarnation through his own loving presence. Through his memory of childhood, through the gentleness with which he held his own childhood feelings, Mister Rogers provided a comfort much greater than "Don't cry, don't be afraid," or even "Just let on that you don't care." God cared, Fred believes, enough to be among us and to feel every human feeling, and so Fred worked hard to be with children and their feelings, to explain and alleviate, when possible, but more importantly, to take them seriously – as seriously as God becoming human (Tuttle, p. 14).

Rogers longed for children to develop trust and a sense of self-worth early on in their lives. In a radio broadcast he produced in 1976 for *The Protestant Hour*, Rogers said,

> Christianity to me is a matter of being accepted as we are. Jesus certainly wasn't concerned about people's station in life or what they looked like or whether they were perfect in behavior or feeling. How often in the New Testament we read of Jesus's empathy for those people who felt their own lives to be imperfect, and the marvelous surprise and joy when they sensed his great acceptance (Tuttle, p. 24).

Rogers wrote in 1979, "When we hear the word that we are not lovable … we are *not* hearing the word of God. No matter how unlovely, how impure, or weak or false we may feel ourselves to be, all through the ages God has still called us lovable" (Tuttle, pp. 24-25). In fact, he believed "love is at the heart of everything. Whether it's learning or relationships, love is the heart of everything. Love or the lack of it" ("Won't You Be My Neighbor?" 2018).

"The Word became flesh and made his dwelling among us. We have seen his glory, the glory of the one and only Son, who came from the Father, full of grace and truth" (John 1:14).

Psychology of a Childhood Confessor

Fred Rogers never forgot his own childhood experience of being accepted by his grandfather's unwavering love and affirmation. Because of this, he was able to listen to hear the tender, sometimes anxious, yet beautiful hearts of children. A cameraman who worked on *Mister Rogers' Neighborhood* remembers Fred's response to children lining up to talk to him wherever he went. "I never once heard Fred say, 'Get this kid out of here!' I sure would have," he recounts.

Tuttle describes Rogers' psychology further:

> Fred seems to have craved affirmation – both human and divine – throughout his life … [while] filming a segment for the program … as usual, people approached Fred in droves, and at first, the producer tried to keep them away from him, but every time she turned around, there was Mister Rogers putting his arms around someone, or wiping the tears off someone's cheek, or passing around the picture of someone's child, or getting on his knees to talk to a child. After a while, [the producer] just rolled her eyes and gave up, because it's always like this with Mister Rogers, because the thing that people don't understand about him is that he's *greedy* for this – greedy for the grace that people offer him (Tuttle, p. 25).

In the documentary film, Rogers' wife, Joanne, describes how she and Fred both grew up in families where they were not allowed to be angry. When explaining how her husband made all the voices for the puppets in the Land of Make-Believe, she claims Fred was most clearly seen and heard in the voice of the puppet Daniel Striped Tiger. "Fred Rogers *was* Daniel Striped Tiger!" she exclaims ("Won't You Be My Neighbor?" 2018).

Rogers, himself, once stated it was easier for him to let Daniel Tiger speak what went on inside of him, even though the distance between his mouth and the face of his puppet was short. Daniel

Tiger was Rogers' confessor, and a confessor to countless children also. Daniel Tiger speaks confessions such as this:

> I wonder if I'm a mistake? I'm not like anyone else. When I am asleep or even awake, sometimes I dream I'm just a fake. I'm not like anyone else.
>
> Lady Betty Aberlin responds to Daniel, "I think you are just fine as you are. I really must tell you, I do like the person you are becoming. When you are sleeping, when you are waking, you're not a fake, you're no mistake. You are my friend. I think you are fine exactly the way you are."
>
> Daniel asks, "The way I look?"
>
> Lady Aberlin answers, "Yes."
>
> "The way I talk?" he questions.
>
> "Yes," Lady replies.
>
> "The way I love?" prodding further.
>
> "Yes, especially that!" she affirms. (*Won't You Be My Neighbor?*, 2018)

This is what Fred Rogers needed to hear himself, and the message he wanted to tell all children.

"Truly I tell you, anyone who will not receive the kingdom of God like a little child will never enter it." And he took the children in his arms, placed his hands on them and blessed them (Mark 10:15-16).

Children's Need for Confessors . . . Confessors' Need for Children

Rogers pictures parents in the role of childhood confessors in his book on parenting.

> Children help to open our eyes with their natural curiosity. Since they don't have much of a sense of cause-and-effect or what's real and what isn't, they're full of creative interpretations and misinterpretations! What a special time for parents who are listening to their children's questions and conclusions! Children give us the great gift of a fresh, intriguing look at the world . . . Young children are full of feelings, and those feelings are often hard to express and hard to control. Children are not born with self-control. They need a lot of help as they try to figure out appropriate ways to express their feelings ... In their social world, they're learning what it means to be a friend, but they're still egocentric. They aren't yet able to see things from someone else's perspective, so sharing and getting along with others can be difficult ... young children are looking for parents for help in understanding the world, their relationships with others, and their perplexing inner feelings . . . You already have one of the most important resources built into your parenting: *you were a child once yourself!* Those memories are still there, and they can bubble up within us just from seeing or hearing something that our children say or do. Since we were children once, the roots for our empathy are already planted within us. We've known what it was like to feel small and powerless, helpless and confused. When we can feel something of what our children might be feeling, it will help us begin to figure out what our children need from us. Each time we work those struggles, we have another chance of coming to

a greater mastery over them when we become parents; just being involved in our children's struggles evokes another reworking in us. As parents we have another chance to grow. And we can bring our children understanding, comfort, and hopefulness when they need this kind of support, then they are more likely to grow into adults who can find these resources within themselves later on (Rogers, pp. 14-15).

Listening, understanding their world, their perplexing feelings, knowing what it's like to be a child needing comfort and hope: these are all aspects of the childhood confessor.

Another revisiting of Mister Rogers, in addition to the pair of recent films, is the podcast, "Finding Fred." In Episode 5, "Invisible to the Eye," host Carvel Wallis notes that Rogers frequently quoted *The Little Prince*:

It is only with the heart that one can see rightly. What is essential is invisible to the eye." Sometimes the most important feelings that we have, the most essential ones, are the quiet, nearly invisible ones. The tiny feeling of regret that nags us when we think we might be hurting someone. The small tingle that we feel when we see someone we love. And maybe when we're children, these feelings are louder in us, more intense. The thing is, as children we don't yet know which feelings are to be ignored … [or] the ones that are important …We count on the adults in our lives to help sort that out as we go. So, what happens when the adults who are supposed to be teaching us are unable to listen with the heart – when they don't pay attention to how we're feeling or what we need? What happens when adults can't help us because their lives are too busy or too loud? Or too full of fear? When we are left alone with feelings we don't understand or know what to do with? What kind of world does that make for all of us? And what kind of world would we have if we were better at listening to the cues of children – especially the children that live somewhere inside of us?" (Saint-Exupery, 2000)

There are problems we stuff into the basements and attics of our souls, many from our childhood. The heart is not able to listen, the noise is too loud, feelings are indistinguishable in the recesses of our inner lives. A confessor steps into the aloneness of another and is fully present the way that Fred Rogers is with children.

Fred Rogers is a Confessor ... How did I miss this?

Children need confessors too, no matter how old one might be.

> *What follows is a Confession from one of the ministers I coach, Chris Manley in Chattanooga, Tennessee. Indeed, this chapter is his contribution. Many of the ministers I coach carry a deep or traumatic childhood wound. Allow the story of Chris' childhood confession to help us hear what we do not hear and see what we do not see.*

I am a child from a broken home, my parents divorcing when I was 15. My parents love me deeply. They did not intend to wound me, but they were wounded themselves. So, I have some mold in my emotional basement and junk cramped in the attic of my soul. Although unintentional, their wounds wounded me, especially in my early childhood.

In a way, we are all little kids walking around in ill-fitting clothes we pulled out of our parent's closet. We pretend we know what we are doing. We present ourselves as grown-ups, able to handle life. Now, don't get me wrong, the little kid inside who learned to survive is a badass! At the same time, we often run scared fearing our survival techniques will not work this time. Subtly, even to ourselves, we perpetually evaluate each person crossing our path, wondering whether they might be a means of healing or further wounding.

My mother grew up in a religiously oppressive home. She had to perform to receive love from her parents. Consequently, she believes she must perform to be loved by God as well. She has wrestled with this ever since. She lives with a palatable fear of relational rejection, not to mention an anger you dare not cross.

My father grew up in an emotionally abusive home. His father was abused also as a child and was emotionally absent, always around but never there. When my family would visit my grandparents as a child, I remember sitting on the floor near the locked door of my grandfather's office, just longing to be invited in. But that never happened.

My father ate his pain, literally, rather than acknowledging it. He became a food addict. I am not sure if he was aware how his growing obesity affected those around him, or if he was purposefully creating distance between himself and others. But his obesity definitely pushed others away. It kept us from enjoying experiences we saw other families around us having.

From years of mistreatment of his body and neglect of his emotional inner life, my father swelled to almost 500 lbs. After gastric-bypass surgery, he lost over 200 lbs. But the years of avoiding what was molding in his emotional basement and bending the beams of his attic of his soul, expressed in his physical weight resulted in a fall, causing a brain injury. Now he lives in a long-term rehabilitation facility. My father *waited too long to address what he needed to confess.* My father needed a confessor to share his pain and deep need of being loved. In 2021, he passed away and was healed in the heaven he longed for.

Who I am is largely a result of my father eating his emotions rather than offering them to me; and my mother looking to me to fill the emotional deficiency she lacked from her childhood and marriage. It is true what they say – "we play the hand we were dealt." My parents were dealt a weak hand from which to play.

Being a child with normal needs who was required to fulfill my parents' emotional needs, forced me into the role of an adult when I should have been figuring out what it was like to be a kid. This stunted my emotional development and caused me to think I could handle anything. Being required to carry the weight of the emotional needs of my family, made me think I was more mature than I really was. I developed the sense I was on my own in life.

From my mom, I absorbed her wound of, "I must perform to receive and keep the love of others." I assume my measure of love will get me the measure I need in return. My love makes my family happy and okay – which is the only way I am happy and okay. This messaging led me to believe I am loved for the needs I meet.

Because of my family wound, I adopted sinful patterns. I can be insecure, manipulative, self-centered, controlling, and not fully present with others. Like George Bailey, the protagonist from *It's A Wonderful Life*, I do not appreciate the incredible gift of the present because I'm longing for a future dream-scenario I must work hard to attain.

Understanding my story has led me to love and understand my parents while also acknowledging the ways they wounded me. When people are hurting, they often hurt other people. Part of addressing our wounds is confession. When we acknowledge and confess our wounds, we can be a confessor to other wounded people.

As an adult, when my wife and I hit a particular crisis point in our lives, my wife pleaded with me to address my past wounds playing into our present. I began to realize I was an emotional adolescent in many ways. No one could do the work of my inner life but me. I began to see how I have lived my life as a lost kid at a carnival, running to each adult near me, hoping to look up and find my mother or father. That never really worked, and it wasn't working now. So, I began to explore the wounds ruling my inner life.

The real heroes in my story are my wife and some key confessors in my life, who have pulled me close because of my deep needs. Another confessor came into my life unexpectedly, when my eight-year-old daughter stumbled upon a TV program on Amazon Prime I had not watched in many years. I grew up loving it. She said, "Daddy, can we watch this show?"

"Absolutely!" I reply.

About halfway through the episode she chose, I look down at her sitting cross-legged on the floor soaking in the experience and notice a big tear flowing down her cheek. She was making no sound. Something was stirring in her. As I glanced back up at the screen, I felt tears flowing down my cheek also.

My daughter and I were both experiencing kindness in our inner being. Someone was piercing through the television screen into our souls—touching the very core of our deepest longing. This confessor made us both feel appreciated for who we are and liked exactly as we are. Can you guess who it is? Mister Rogers. Mister Rogers became my confessor.

Because our wounds often come from deep needs not being met earlier in our lives, maturity is a slow and painful process of coming to own our wounds rather than being owned by them. It is the process of discovering the unhealthy ways we try to meet our longings, or, as a friend of mine says, "Learning to have coffee with your demons." Identifying the demons alongside the deep needs of every image-bearer is an essential step toward healthier patterns. This allows us to have compassion on ourselves, accepting who we are.

It's difficult to show compassion on others when you have not practiced on yourself. Knowing how weak we truly are helps us see others' weaknesses alongside our own. This enables us to offer ourselves to others honestly and vulnerably. This is the role of the confessor.

The role of the confessor is a guide, a fellow traveler who walks alongside others who are hurting, listening for what they really need. A confessor seeks to hear the frequency of desire and engages in the messiness of unmet desires while affirming them "just the way they are."

Mr. Rogers filled that space as a confessor for a generation of children.

Chapter 8: The Confessor's Inner World

I own a black truck. I love how it shines when I wash and polish it and it reflects like a mirror. It makes me wonder whether black is brighter than any other color. But when black paint gets dirty it shows every speck of dirt. Even a brand-new truck can look old and tired if rained on or dirty from normal road grit. There's no hiding the dirt. To own a black truck means, you might want to commit to washing it. Often.

Confessors are a little like my black truck – there's no hiding the muck. To be a confessor means you must first learn how to keep the space in your own soul. A confessor must continually be the *confessee*. This enables the confessor to be a mirror for others.

Confessors offer a safe, no-pressure laboratory for a soul to tell and explore its secrets. It is interesting to watch a *confessee* begin to observe him/herself telling. For instance, the sweet spot of a tattoo interview comes when the owner discovers what is underneath the tattoo right in front of you! Often, the Image of God is writing a message to the owner of the tattoo. The confessor not only gets to watch but also experiences the wonder of being the "listener who hears" with the ears of God. I believe God's Spirit anoints the confessor to be a part of another soul's unburdening.

Come to me, all you who are weary and burdened, and I will give you rest. Take my yoke upon you and learn from me, for I am gentle and humble in heart, and you will find rest for your souls. For my yoke is easy and my burden is light (Matthew 11:28-30).

Our Need to "Wash the Car"

Yet being a part of another soul's unburdening is soul-taxing work. It's hard being a mirror to the muck and not come away at least a little scathed. Confessors are never completely untouched by the confession, nor should they be. They are called to step into sacred space and expose their own souls as they help unburden another's.

Confessors must be especially aware of malevolence. There are spiritual forces of willful, dark, and unspeakable evil at work in the world. My friends in the State Department study the evils of ISIS, genocide, and war crimes. People who witness such atrocities need to tell someone. When a confessor hears the worst of the worst, he/she must bring it to God Himself and seek His just care. Sometimes there are things we cannot un-see or erase from our minds. Rarely is the confessor given the option to say, "Let me stop you right there, I don't want to know anymore." Sometimes the evil is so black and dark, the confessor loses his breath, or even the sense of God being in charge.

My eighty-six-year-old friend, Toby, has been around the block enough times to let go of all the things that pricked him in the night. Or so I thought. One day, Toby looks at me and says, "You know I still wonder, Pastor Al." Toby was inviting me to step with him into the "confessor's booth in the *wild*".

"Wonder about what, my friend?" I ask.

"My parents were extremely poor. In our home, food was a luxury, not a given. Four kids in the family were one too many mouths to feed. My parents chose me, Pastor Al. I went to live with a distant relative six hundred miles away from the age of five. I never saw my family again …Why did they choose me to be the one to leave? Did I eat too much? Was it something I did or said?" he asks, not expecting an answer.

I sit in silence with Toby, who needed to talk about a memory from when he was just five years old. I mourn with him. I reach out to hug this 86-year-old boy and say, "I am so, so sorry."

In Chapter 3, we considered the role of the "sin-eater" as portrayed in *The Green Mile*. John Coffey, though innocent, accepts death as freedom from the sins he still carries on behalf of others. It's ironic – the sin of another bringing him to a place of release. And yet, his only recourse for freedom was death. This character illustrates the confessor's need to re-open, re-enlighten, and clean out the dark acids inside the soul. The weight of another's pain and sin collects in the soul of the confessor like an overstuffed garage. It must be routinely cleaned out.

In "The Two Towers" – the second volume of *The Lord of the Rings* trilogy – the wizard, Saruman, a dark evil menace who craves power and destruction, possesses King Theoden's body and mind. Once a strong king boldly fighting evil, Theoden becomes weak, old, and tormented. Grima Wormtongue, the King's snake-like advisor, ensures that King Theoden remains oppressed by his many burdens.

Gandalf hears of King Theoden's possession by Saruman and hatches a plot for the King's rescue. Gandalf enters the King's chambers leaning on his staff as if he needs it to walk. Once inside, Gandalf finds King Theoden blinded with petrified skin. Gandalf throws back his hood and waves his staff/wand, but Saruman does not release his captive king easily. Gandalf and Saruman are equally matched. As Gandalf redoubles his command and continues waving his wand, he wrests Theoden from Saruman's evil grip. After the exorcism, Theoden regains his youthful strength and appearance. The once-burdened king now is restored to lead his kingdom once more. (Two Towers, 2002)

Gandalf could not have defeated Saruman without being completely focused and determined. Maybe there are so few confessors because the space inside gets filled with our own darkness. Most people cannot take in any more than their own anxieties. The quiet space needed to hear confession becomes drowned out by the drumbeat of our own pain. It becomes impossible to focus on anything let alone a *confessee* needing a safe space to confess.

Perhaps anxiety and mental illness creep in because we need cleaning at least as often as my black truck? As Jesus says to the Pharisees, it's easier to clean the outside of the cup than the inside. If we do not learn how to clean the inside of the cup, to "wash the car" of our souls, at best, we may end up on autopilot by our mid-thirties. Many of the ministers with whom I partner have done this. Initially, they boldly move into the *wild*. They listen well inside the church too. But then their own souls grow heavy – too heavy and dirty to mirror another soul.

"No," said Peter, "you shall never wash my feet." Jesus answered, "Unless I wash you, you have no part with me" (John 13:8).

Ways to "Wash the Car"

After venturing into the role of the confessor, you must then find the time and space to be able to recover from hearing, seeing, and feeling the weight of evil. You must wash your black truck.

How do our souls, tormented by darkness, hurt, fear, and past offences, become unburdened? King Jesus assures us His yoke is easy and His burden is light (Mathew 11:30). At the same time, when we do heavy soul-plowing with another, our own souls, minds, and body need Jesus' gentle care.

I cannot tell you I know the right way for each confessor to "wash the car." For some, it can be a challenging task to become unburdened – to recover, reboot, and even be ready to listen deeper. We all have our own complex, collected darkness. We each have unique demons, struggles from our formative years, and dynamics passed on generationally. Yet I will offer what is helping me in this journey.

Breathing

Yes, breathing. Physically. Inhale, exhale.

Now, I promise to not go all Eastern mystic on you. But I am going to Genesis 2. When God creates man from the dust of the ground, He breathes into him "the breath of life." Ordinarily a body cannot stay alive for more than two minutes without air. To live, the body must breathe. God also designs humans with a mind and body in sync. I suspect breathing is the yoga of the soul. Okay, so I've gone a tad Eastern, but stay with me. Something special happens when one is allowed to breathe in deeply and breathe out slowly. Our blood pressure goes down and tensed-up muscles loosen. Anyone can do one good inhale and one good exhale.

I ask some of the ministers I coach to put an outdoor chair in the trunk of their car. Now, these are brilliant people, smarter and more spiritual than me. So, as I coach, I am careful with their dignity. I ask permission and make suggestions. One phrase I use often is, "I get to say anything I want, and you get to ignore anything I say."

The first thing I work with them on is seeing, imagining, or driving to a park or river with trees nearby. As a start, I try to guide them to be able to find solitude within twenty minutes to breathe. One good inhale and one good exhale in twenty minutes is a success! A third of the ministers say this is the most life changing thing we do in our residency. I ask them to do it once a week, and, by the end of the twelve months of our partnership, every day.

Many conversations and new ways of thinking stem from this breathing exercise. I suspect the soul that "stores the confessions" begins to find space by breathing. The confessor must make space to give these stored memories and confessions back to God. Only God can know, embrace, and answer the confessions a confessor carries. If a confessor falls into the delusion that he/she is strong enough to hear and hold the confessions of a world full of broken hearts, he/she will quickly become disillusioned.

Nature

In my own tribe of ministers, we attract mostly left-brainers. To solve problems, left-brainers believe, we must discover more information and insight. They think that the more Biblically and theologically precise we become, the power of understanding truth alone will make us … more right.

The problem is we are more than left-brain beings. Memorizing, reasoning, comprehending, and categorizing all take place in the left-brain. This is good and needed, but the left brain also needs rest and balance. So, left-brainers developed a concept called – a retreat! The problem is, a left-brain retreat typically gathers other tired left-brainers to listen to a left-brain speaker, occasionally interrupted by a nature break in order to go out and think some more.

Now, there is left-brain precision in nature, for sure. The migration routes of sea turtles are shockingly precise. But we should not miss out on the unexplainable wonder in nature! The monkeys play and swing through trees because they can. A butterfly, a flying flower, delights in where the winds will take her. The elephant trumpets loudly when another wants to play and sprays water through its trunk!

The right brain experiences beauty, exploration, feeling, imagination, and mystery. Nature exercises the right side of our brain! God made everything in nature, in part, to ignite our imagination, to create heart-stopping awe, and to massage our souls. This is how God responds restfully on the seventh day! Nature inspires a soul-sized wonder at creation. Every mountain calls out to be seen or scaled. Every ocean invites wading, swimming, or sailing. Trees offer shade, bear fruit, or invite being climbed or simply admired.

Big old trees move me too. Sometimes, I just sit with them wondering what storms they survived, who they met, or what sound waves have they stored inside? Maybe old trees are the confessors of nature?

I also love Labrador Retrievers. These dogs simply know how to be. Each of my chocolate Labs has been like a family member. (Sometimes I give them a "vote" in family matters when it works to my advantage.) They always know their job: to retrieve. They especially love retrieving a ball or stick thrown into a river. When they aren't retrieving, they wait to retrieve, sometimes even sleeping with the ball in their mouth.

When I watch my dogs, love being themselves and doing what they do, it begins to trickle down inside me. It's hard to be depressed around a labrador retriever. Labs don't get depressed. When a dog's body grows tired from retrieving, the dog becomes loving. My labs never stop loving me. Could God love me as much as my lab? I often think, "Nope, not possible!"

Want to be a healthy confessor? Go roll in nature. Walk in it, breathe it, observe it, let it sleep in your bed. Let a current take you down a river. God designed nature for mankind – to be life-giving, healing and imagination igniting. Let Him kiss you with love through nature!

Play

When I see a group of preschoolers running around in a circle, falling into each other, and laughing with high-pitched giggles, I see the heart of God. God creates play. Left brainers have a hard time with this too.

Play is release. It's excitement for the soul, silly joy with other humans or creation. Adults pay large sums of money to rediscover play like they experienced as a child. But simply playing with little children can do the trick. You can be silly, make them laugh, roll on the ground, play hide-and-seek with a two-year-old who thinks hiding is the same as shutting their eyes. Children are what kept me in the brick-and-mortar church for years. One of them called me "Aster Pal" in front of the whole congregation! Years of silly giggles followed with the children as I would feign being mad at being called "Aster Pal" and the little child would shout it even louder!

Play can be found in board games, card games, surfing, guys, or girls' nights out once a month, and a host of other activities you enjoy. For me, dancing helps most. (Please don't visualize me dancing, as your therapist might need a therapist.) In high school I went to a dance class as a gym elective. It changed my life. To move your body to music in sync with another is creative play. There is the joy I see reflected in my dance partner's face!

After I went to seminary and started a church, I didn't dance for about 10 years. Then I went to Samburu, Kenya. When I declared, "God is great," the Kenyans would dance and chant, "God is Great!" I began to speak in a cadence allowing space for their response and movements. This was so much fun, I asked the Chief, "Could we take a dance break?"

The chief replied, "I am not sure God would be pleased."

I countered, "I think God would be okay with it if the chief agreed!"

Oh, did we dance and dance and dance! Something released in my soul!

When I returned home to Virginia/DC, I took East and West coast swing dance lessons. Deb and I are regular dancers now. It's play! It opens something silly yet meaningful with others.

Play helps the confessor create space and health in his own soul. What is your play? Your secret play you have always longed to get to? What is holding you back?

Find your Confessor

Finding your own confessor might take a while. Is there someone already in your life who is a confessor or could be? Becoming a confessor requires not only hearing deeply but also telling your own secrets of the soul. As I have been saying, confessors need space to unstuff their souls to make room for listening to others. The best confessors are those who confess often and deeply. Our souls are less noisy when we release a secret, offense, hope, or hurt into the ears of another. You need someone who can suspend judgment, empathize, and strengthen *your* spirit in order to do this for others.

When my children were growing up, one would fall, scrape up a knee, leg, or elbow. I would pick the hurt one up, say, "I'm so sorry," and send him/her back off to play – mission accomplished. But mom was their confessor. Hours after a scrape happened, each child, needing her to know what happened, would hurt all over again while describing it.

We still need someone like this in our lives. We never get beyond it. It's just that, as an adult, the wounds we need to tell a confessor are less visible. I have a few dear friends and mentors in my life. Something happens inside me when they let me tell what's happening within me. Something gets released, healed, and, sometimes, a new space opens inside me. A confessor cannot be an island to him/ herself. Confessors need confessors.

Health

The role of the confessor is like an extreme sport: it takes a tremendous amount of healthy conditioning. The older we get, the harder this conditioning becomes. But it's not just an issue of physically aging. The toll of experiencing and hearing others' pent-up hurts, anger, and offences can zap emotional and physical energy. The body knows the secrets we internalize.

Most pastors and leaders must deal with unrealistic expectations, whether from themselves or others. Churches and other organizations are fragile political-psychological entities. There is the chronic conflictual person, sometimes a legion of them. There are the board meetings where no one can agree. There is the big giver who uses money to control. Typically, church leaders face the headwinds of conflict alone and, instead of looking for a confessor, they internalize the stress.

Most of us feign optimism. We acknowledge God's sovereign control. We know a redemptive process is going on. And we know we are the chief among sinners. But still, we act like we can bear our burdens alone. Internalizing our stress impacts our health directly as it creates chemicals that are detrimental to our bodies. It impacts us indirectly as we turn to unhealthy crutches and addictions to bear the load.

My own health suffered from drinking too much coffee. The caffeine high/buzz takes a toll on sleep. Obesity can be a problem in a pastor's world because much of our meeting people is around food. Sometimes we become emotional comfort eaters. Confessors must take time to care for our bodies. Otherwise, our bodies and souls cannot hold the weights, burdens, pain, and darkness within ourselves or others.

Other things I keep an eye on:

1. When I get annoyed or judgmental towards people in my parish, it's time to get alone.

2. When I get emotionally distant or indifferent toward people I normally love with ease, it's time to get alone.

3. Live as a lover. I find myself telling the people in my bar and network, "I love you" because I do. Discernment is needed on saying this, indeed, but living as a lover is the only way to go.

4. I tell my people in my parish, "I need you more than you need me." Often people laugh, but it's true. The affection and care people have given me, and my wife, is remarkable!

5. Finally, keep an eye on your idol(s). What's that thing you must have? What is that secret obsession? What owns too much of your mind and heart, or haunts you when you sleep? Sometimes, it's the simple, good things we want or demand more than God.

On my way home from listening to my friend Toby's story, I stop at the river, pull my chair out, and watch my Lab swim with wild abandon. It helps me.

Confessors must wash the car, keep our core strong, and make space and for our next assignment in Listening to Hear. You are like my black truck – in need of cleaning in order to shine.

The Confessor's inner world ... like my black truck ... How did I miss this?

Chapter 9: Habits of the Image of God

On a Balian beach in Indonesia, I take a writing sabbatical. I rent a treehouse in this remote and quiet paradise where the surf soothes my soul.

My first discovery is my nearest neighbors 400 yards away, a little couple, very elderly, who live in a tiny house. The two greet me with smiles and hand-folded bows, and I return them. I watch the husband swim in the river by the ocean each day, to catch fish with traps, made of palm branches, for his wife to cook when he gets home. He cuts coconuts and mangos from wild trees.

At one point, I give them a bag of rice. Their joyful appreciation becomes a heart changer for me. I feel like I am stepping back in time. So many of my first-world desires surface – a newer car, straighter teeth, the latest smartphone, and a hotter latte. How does this couple fill my soul with their smiles when they have nothing?

This leads to a second discovery in my tropical paradise: the Image of God travels. God's image wanders in space and time. The Image of God is genius-like, hidden, coming out when it wants to, and looking around. The grinning Cheshire cat from Lewis Carroll's *Alice in Wonderland* teaches Alice the Wonderland rules, but it also has a habit of disappearing (Carroll, 1865). So too, the habits of the Image of God seem to disappear just as much as they show us the wiring of creation.

In my confessor journey, I grow in deeper respect of the Image of God every day. It's not so much that I discover the Image of God in other people as that God's image discovers and signals itself to me. Perhaps the Image of God in me sends a signal of dignity and respect to His image in another person. As I sense His signal, trust, introspection, and vulnerability begin to beat along with my heart.

> Then God said, "Let us make mankind in our image, in our likeness, so that they may rule over the fish in the sea and the birds in the sky, over the livestock and all the wild animals, and over all the creatures that move along the ground." So, God created mankind in his own image, in the image of God he created them; male and female he created them (Genesis 1:26-27).

What is "The Image of God?"

A myrmecologist studies ants: their ways, habits, secrets, survival skills, and "operating systems." Given that there are 12,000 species of ants, this is quite an extensive field of study (Myrmecology, 2002).

How do ants learn ant behaviors anyway? Is there a common internal code with which every ant is born? Likely so. The common internal code with which every human is born is called the Image of God.

Where is the Image of God? What are its habits? When do we know we are in its presence? When a baby is conceived and begins a tiny heartbeat, is the Image of God beginning to beat too? When a person dies, does God's Image go first or last?

These questions, unanswerable as they are, can and should transport us to new ways of thinking. Our imagination can stretch us into a place of suspecting things we can't quite prove. It moves us into a space of intuition that extends from the Image of God within us.

As I walk in the *wild*, outside the brick-and-mortar church, I find a common ground in the inner person. This is an entry point where I begin to hear something old and new, distant yet present. The common ground all people share is the Image of God. A confessor begins to study, hear, know, and enjoy the signals extending from the Image of God in others.

A confessor studies the inner workings of the Image of God. He hears messages not fully verbalized and coming in spurts and pauses. A certain set of "laws" or "axioms" come with being human, no matter a person's mental health status. The confessor discovers a baseline understanding about the Law of God in image-bearers, even if faintly. This Law is in the mind and heart. It identifies beauty, innocence, revenge, duplicity, authenticity, and love. The confessor detects these inner dynamics as "she protests too much." That is, the more a person protests, the thing being protested often becomes truer than initially realized. The presenter rushes into a space with proofs to show the strength of his counterpoint. The confessor lives a life of patient waiting and is rewarded.

Through listening, staying still, and waiting for it, the Confessor begins to sense the Laws of God operative in His image bearers. For instance, the most basic law for human interaction is the Sixth Commandment. It is also a universal law of humanity: "Do not murder." To violate it, even in wartime, sets off tremors of trauma in those who kill someone. How many veterans live out their later years with their conscience replaying over and over the death of another? The law of God is written deeply within both the conscious and subconscious being of the Image of God. Even if we become angry enough to wish someone dead, rarely will we carry it out. And neither should we.

> I am worn out calling for help; my throat is parched. My eyes fail, looking for my God. You, God, know my folly; my guilt is not hidden from you (Psalm 69:3, 5).

What Does the Image of God Do?

The Image of God thinks and watches. Everyone observes and tries to figure out the world we live in. Like a submarine captain who peers through a periscope quietly in the ocean, stealthily submerged away from perceived enemies, we want to see all around us. We want to know what's going on, how it all makes sense, and how it impacts us.

I suspect something inside of each person (namely, the Image of God) is thinking alongside of a person's conscious thoughts. This "back and forth" dynamic of two thinkers is the common ground for the "seeing and hearing" confessor. The Image of God sends messages to its owner. A confessor is one who listens to a soul that is processing internal conversations, out loud. My experience in my parish bar is the conscience gets a little freer after two drinks! I don't know what to make of this theologically, but I see it again and again.

When the back-and-forth dynamic is at play, and a confessor enters soul space, a person's first inclination often is to deflect. For instance, when I ask, "Does your tattoo have a story?" The most frequent response is, "Nah, just a bad drunk night, man." That's a cover story, a decoy! The actual story beneath the tattoo may be a still-born daughter or some other hidden hurt wanting to stay close to its owner and not tell a stranger with unknown motives. Is the Image of God writing a message in and through a tattoo to its owner? I think so.

The Image of God also sends and picks up signals. Currently, I am researching the question, "How do people with a mental disability receive faith? Do they have an antenna?" Some argue it is easy to project anything you want on an unpredictable mind or mysterious handicap. Others, who work with people who have mental disabilities, find evidence of thought, communication, and signaling that cannot be dismissed. Humans, even with mental disabilities, have antennae picking up and sending signals. I believe this is the Image of God at home in a soul whether mildly or severely mentally challenged. The confessor discerns God's image in the *confessee* with disabilities as he or she communicates with the outside world.

Helen Keller was born blind and deaf. Helen was *not* mentally disabled though it would have been easy to think so because of her physical disabilities. Yet people in her life persevered in getting through to Helen. As these people explored, much more was discovered beneath the surface in her soul, even though it appeared hidden in her blindness and deafness. She learned to communicate by putting her fingers on the speaker's lips and her thumb on their larynx. Her teacher, Annie Sullivan, signed books and lectures into Helen's hand. Eventually, she graduated with a Bachelor of Arts degree *cum laude* from Radcliffe College in 1904. Helen Keller also received honorary doctoral degrees from Temple, Harvard, Glasgow, Delhi, and Johannesburg Universities (Keller, 2001).

Why did Helen Keller find a place in the world? *Her teacher listened.* The Image of God in disabled people may very well offer insights on the Image of God in all people. A confessor can learn to hear the Image of God signaling within a mentally disabled soul if we will dare to listen.

Not only does the Image of God think and watch, pick up, and send signals, but *the Image of God speaks.* It can express its hurts. "Pastor Al, did your God allow the coronavirus to spread? Huh? You can keep your God, Pastor Al!" The Image of God in my friend Bill is telling me what hurts. A Presenter would argue the point. A confessor says, "I get it Bill; I get it."

For years Zach observed me in my parish, our bar. I observe Zach making his crazy bird noise ("Ca cawww, cacawwwwwww") in response to different bands playing in the bar. It seems a little more than a bit odd for a man of 66. But we never talk.

One day, I walk up to the bar for my usual iced tea. The bartender sees me and places it in my hand without me asking. On this day, Zach speaks to me. "So, Pastor Al, how are you?"

If Zach had not used my name, I would assume he was talking to someone other than me. Yet, I answer, "I'm fine. Thanks, friend!"

"My name is Zach. You're a beloved figure around here, Pastor Al."

"I like to think so!" I reply.

And suddenly, Zach turns into a relatable, intelligent person! He tells me about his business, his family, and his drinking problem. Turns out I knew about his business but did not know Zach, the "cacawwww" guy, owned it.

Zach takes another sip of his drink, then says, "My father was a super, super religious guy. Everything was about the church. I had to "tow the line." When church membership came up when I was 13, my dad told me to get ready, and I said 'No.' He beat the devil out of me. I thought about running away, but, at 13, that wasn't the greatest idea. I played the game, and, at 18, I was out of there! Pastor Al…it didn't all add up. Is three quarters of the population is going to hell? Is the only way to go to this one Heaven through Jesus? What about all the other religions, Pastor Al? I saw my father a few more times after I left but not many. We never did become father and son again," Zach reflected.

Then he asks, "Pastor Al, did you do some trick on me to tell you all that stuff? If you did, could you teach it to me?"

"Zach I'm sorry—so sorry," I say. "Great seeing you! I'm sure we will talk again. Thank you for sharing your story. I see you differently now." As I walk away, I know this is the beginning of many more conversations. Now when I hear, "ca ca ca caaawwww," I wonder if Zach is calling out to someone else in addition to the band.

> He has walled me in so I cannot escape; he has weighed me down with chains. Even when I call out or cry for help, he shuts out my prayer. He has barred my way with blocks of stone; he has made my paths crooked (Lamentations 3:7-9).

Final Thoughts

Often Christians want to give an answer or defend God from people's accusations stemming from their pain. But accusations often manifest themselves in the Image of God who longs to tell someone what hurts. Will you become a confessor who listens, holds, and hears some more…and watch faith and healing stir?

The Image of God … sending signals … looking for a confessor … How did I miss this?

Chapter 10: How Now?

"How now brown cow?" began as an elocution exercise and developed into an entertaining children's poetry book. Hearing an answer to, "How now brown cow?" only happens in the imagination. Yet, as we come to the last chapter in The Confessor, the question arises, "How now?" Answering this question will take some imagination, some re-imagining. How do we walk through the world in this time and space?

We live in a world straining under the pollution of our food chain and natural habitats. Crowded cities take a toll both on the planet and our souls. Overpopulation is like a petri dish with the Coronavirus pandemic. With our changing climate, we are left to wonder whether this is an anomaly or the result of the abuse of our planet. You choose; either answer is not a good one.

More people live on this earth today than ever before. Yet social scientists warn us loneliness has become epidemic, and maybe even pandemic. Social media fixation has even created a demand for waterproof smartphones to take into the shower, pool, or hot tub! First-world problems such as obesity and opioid addictions evidence the emotional struggles of our era. Our world grows more and more anxious; fear and uncertainty keep us from having a good night's rest and steal the will to get out of bed the next morning. Meanwhile, the world is getting angrier. We shout at each other, even in church. But few are hearing one other. We are at a global tipping point.

The culture of the American church is experiencing a tipping point too. Eighty-five percent of the population is not coming back into our religious structures and buildings. Institutions like the church are being marginalized. Literally and metaphorically, the church occupies "orthodox" real estate, but no one is calling their agent to see, and few want to re-enter. The church's "Building Brain" cultivates a celebrity culture for the successful and undermines a minister's mental health and pastoral calling.

Throughout this book, I plead for a listening, presence-based, confessor mode for the church and its ministers. I believe we have over-presented and misrepresented truth to the point it sounds like platitudes with no substance. As the Apostle Paul adapted to each cultural context in which he entered, so we must adapt and contextualize our way of relating the gospel in our cultural moment.

Our presentation machine is broken. The public walks away while we shout at each other and reinforce our detached subculture. The same becomes an echo chamber where we only hear our own voices. Add "fake news" in our culture, and skepticism heightens toward our truth claims.

If I make you nervous by pitting "proclaim" against "listen" my aim is not to abandon proclaiming, but to ask us to consider whether our listening travels the distance for people to hear what we hope to proclaim. Is there another way to proclaim? Maybe our faithful presence embodies the gospel more meaningfully than our presentations. Maybe our over-marketed culture, where everyone has an angle, makes our presentation feel like one more over-hyped commercial.

If you have made it this far, you may be intrigued, but still not persuaded. Let me have one more shot at convincing you. Shifting our paradigm of ministry will not happen without stepping out from the common expectations of the brick-and-mortar church. Worship, word, and sacrament connect us to the invisible church. They are there to nourish and welcome the convinced.

Far too often, we stay in our buildings using metrics of attendance: aiming for rightness more than righteousness; polishing our performance to satisfy critique from within or "competition" from outside; and emphasizing "corporate" worship so narrowly that we develop a "corporate culture" instead of answering the questions people outside our churches are asking. We create a major danger of missing the tipping point in which we find ourselves! We perpetuate an echo chamber on orthodox real estate where everyone agrees theologically, philosophically, culturally, and even politically.

Perhaps some of the best habits we can practice in order to invigorate Sunday worship are knowing, relating, and listening. Perhaps, by listening to the eighty-five percent who are unlikely to come to our buildings, future generations will soften because we have dared to shift from proclamation only and begun listening to hear.

How might we step in this direction? Let's overview some of what *The Confessor* recommends.

Get into the wild. Leave your Christian conversations for a bit, get off your Christian carpet, and go outside of Christian coffee shops and church buildings. Go somewhere you enjoy where people who probably would never come to your church gather. If you are accustomed to being the center of attention, resist the urge. Be quiet there. Observe. Smile! If you're in the clergy, don't work on your sermon. See whether people will give you their eyes. Acknowledge eye contact non-verbally. Try to imagine what their lives might be like before meeting them. Pray for people based on what you can pick up on about them.

Listen. Chances are good you talk more than you listen. Genesis 1-2 has quite a lot of listening. Nature listens. It's healing. Slow. Be quiet. Breathe. Hear silence. Listen to people with your ears and eyes. See what people are saying with their mouths, eyes, and actions. Introduce yourself and learn their names. When necessary, ask simple questions. Wait for it. Then wait some more. Bite your tongue. We begin at the listening stage of our confessor journey, but the Hearing and Holding stage await our discovery. Pack extra gear, it's going to be a long ride.

Discover. The confessor is an explorer, a researcher, an emotional and spiritual anthropologist. Is this you? Are you willing to take the risk? The confessor is a Scholar Evangelist. His field of study is the soul. Yet, he lets the soul he explores make her own discovery. These discoveries are shared between the *confessee* and confessor. And you protect, care for, and grieve with the *confessee* along the way.

Tattoos. Can we connect with the people in the *wild* where we encounter them? Can we listen patiently enough to hear what's under the tattoo? Opportunity awaits! "I like your tattoo. Can you tell me about it?" Wait for it. Even sharing Skittles may surface something over which you will cry.

Priest. Listen to what a soul wants to confess. Make room in your soul to hear another's words plus even the words they don't know they are saying. You will likely hear a story of deep and profound loss. People struggle to believe God is willing to forgive them. Something in a confessor's forgiveness embodies Christ to the weary and burdened. Vocalizing forgiveness may lead to the hearer to embrace forgiveness. How might the church of shame morph into the church of absolution? Absolution calls out to faith when it peeks out and leads to an experience of forgiveness. Like Jesus with the thief on the cross who expressed mustard seed-size faith, confessors may affirm tiny steps of faith in the *confessee*'s journey into the kingdom to come.

Poet. Develop an ear for the lyrics of confession in today's poets and songsters. Consider how they express each generation's confessions. Watch for and observe people's reactions to songs. Observe the chemistry among a band, their songs, and people's movement to the song. Dance while you're at it. We won't tell anyone!

Creation. Learn from those who love animals. These are tender souls. They reflect God's original and future intent for humans and animals to dwell together in peace. The soul sensitive to animals is very near to the heart of God. If we could treat other humans with the kind of compassion sometimes reserved for animals, we might be onto something!

Mister Rogers. Love them just the way they are – which probably has a lot to do with the childhood wounds and self-protective patterns of survival. Most people, wounded in their formative years, revert to that age emotionally when their pain points are triggered. In those moments they are difficult to love. When an adult behaves like a thirteen-year-old, it's weird. Don't run. Everyone else has. Stay, lean in, discover, and grieve the wound.

Image of God. The Image of God is in everyone, including the non-Christian. Perhaps it is more evident in them than those who flatten God's image in church culture. Look for it. Honor it. Watch it work. Some of my atheist friends provide evidence for God because they reflect his image without acknowledging it. People expect us to begin with their sin. Confessors begin with a person's dignity, power, and glory as God created them.

Final Thoughts

You may have the call to be a Confessor.

If so, your confessional booth is likely not a church building. You may be a tattoo artist, bartender, cigar bar tender, caddy, hair stylist, nutrition or fitness coach, or massage therapist. The confessor is a mysterious role, but an art form for which the world awaits. If you sense this might be you, your gift can grow by present, patient, listening. We must listen to really hear. Play the long game. And watch people pivot in your direction. People will come to you when you have this anointing. A few words well-spoken after many hours of listening can do great things!

The Confessor.

How have we missed this? What's the danger if we keep missing it? But what is there to lose we don't?

How now? In what mode do we function in this age? I suggest it is in the role of the Confessor.

Appendix A: Jean's Story

My friend Jean is from my bar-restaurant. The letter she writes below is her story, her confession. Over the past year, I have listened to hear her story carefully. I let her dictate the pace. She knows about you, the readers of this book, The Confessor. *For Jean, putting her story on paper helps process what she and I talked about. She, like all of us, is a work in progress. Will you practice listening to hear as you read what she writes? Resist the urge to "truth" her. Just hear to understand Jean.*

March 27, 2020

My name is Jean. My name means "God's gracious gift."

I was born because abortion was illegal. My mother had no choice. I did. I had three abortions. This is my story.

My mother was thirty-six with three children who were six, nine, and twelve when I was born. At first, she was angry when she got pregnant with me. She and my father had agreed there would be no more children. Eventually she accepted her condition and was glad. But, after I was born, my mother was overwhelmed. For the first two years of my life my nine-year-old-sister was my caregiver every afternoon when she came home from school. My mother was just too tired for me.

Knowing my mom's tiredness, depression, and medication (Valium) when I was young, I blamed myself. Shame was my point of reference on motherhood. Women were not allowed to have problems and be overwhelmed. unable to raise their own children.

Here is a story I love to tell because I cannot put it into better words:

Two white women were talking between themselves about the children in the Native American tribe. "Can you believe it?" one said to another. "They have children when they are so young and then the entire tribe is responsible for raising them." Another white woman responded, "You'd think the children would feel neglected not knowing who their real mother was."

Two Native American women were talking to each other, and the one woman said to the other "Can you believe it? The white mothers raise their own children in their own house and the children only know just the one mother." The other woman responded, "You'd think the mothers would get very tired after a while."

I was nine when my family moved from the idyllic village of Freeville, New York, to Waverly, New York, a railroad town.

In Waverly, I quickly learned to wear straight-legged pants and not bell-bottoms. Up to that point, I never imagined my body and clothes were a thing to be judged. I wished bell-bottoms would not go out of style, because I had a brand, new pair and I enjoyed the flair and swish when I walked.

I learned to swear. In Waverly you could say "shit" and not fear being struck by lightning. I learned to walk and talk differently -- like I knew stuff. I learned to fit in by not being myself. I was good at being really bad. But if I was really bad, it was clear who I was, and it felt good to know who I was.

This was the 70's when it was cool to be bad. There were drugs, fast cars, and so many ways to get into trouble. I embraced it fully. Like Portia Nelson's poem, "There's a Hole in My Sidewalk," I fell into holes and learned to climb out.

I dated boys – bad boys. The "badder," the better! I was still a child, trying to escape, but I don't know why. I didn't have a lot of support at home, so I went where I was supported. I wish I had been stronger instead of crumbling from the inside out.

Mrs. Moore was the head of physical education and cheerleading at our school. The school was one of the worst in five surrounding counties, but cheerleading was fun! I made the cheer team because I was athletic. I enjoyed the rhythm of using my voice and my body to support and encourage others.

One day, Mrs. Moore sent someone to my locker while I was in the pool. A pack of cigarettes was among my personal belongings. I had stolen them from my mother. Already, Mrs. Moore wanted me off the squad because I was 13 and she knew about my older, high-school drop-out boyfriend from across the tracks. She called me into her office and kicked me off the squad.

I could hear the voice of God saying "I tried to tell you. I did warn you!" It was my voice. I could feel myself shrinking away from the light holding me and giving comfort. Faced with the consequences of my actions, I grew afraid of how I would make it without this light.

I told my mother I got kicked off the team. She was silent, at first, as we were driving. "Are you going to say something?" I asked.

"I'm not impressed with Mrs. Moore." she said. Those words helped me. I realized I was not the only person who made mistakes.

By then, my sisters were in college, my brother was busy, and my parents were tired. They experienced a lot of change moving to a railroad town from our little village above the lake. Without cheerleading, I felt on my own to face the demons in my path. I looked for love, support, and fun in all the wrong places. Art is my thing now, and it has saved me in my life. But back then, there were few creatives in school.

Mrs. Ply, my English teacher, noticed my gift of writing. She went out of her way to show an interest in my poetry. She ensured one of my poems was published in a book for junior and senior high school kids. I felt validated. It was a light in a dark place for me. My poem was about getting lost in fantasy because of reality's harshness. The bog of fantasy was my magical place.

Later in life, I heard she'd fallen in love with a man, quit teaching, and was selling hot dogs by the side of the road with her husband. She wore a bathing suit, sat in a lawn chair, and read a book by the hot dog stand. People would drive by, see her, slow down, then stop to buy a hot dog. They had a booming business! To this day, I believe it was great heroism to defy the status quo and follow her heart.

By the time I was sixteen, I was in a school for juvenile delinquents.

The headmaster warned: "You have f#$%-up, and this is the end of the line. If you don't make it here, you will face a certain and painful future of a diploma-less life full of hardship and drudgery. I can't help you. You must do it yourself. It will be your choice, not mine that saves you."

I loved his speech! What he said was true, direct and to the point.

Our house had ten girls, and there was a boy's house too. We had small classes – six students to one teacher. We lived in rooms in a house with a housemother, named Diane. I admired her – tall, thin, pretty, smart and caring about female delinquents like me. I baby-sat her two little daughters. When they dropped their food on the floor at dinner, I'd make up a song about throwing food! It was a wholesome family, and it made me feel good. Because Diane spoke to me and trusted me, I remembered who I was capable of being.

Also, I loved Mrs. Zen, our typing teacher. She taught like a grandmother, with her heart. She loved us and wanted us to succeed. She showed her love by sharing what mattered to her in her life. In the midst of the women's movement, she was not ashamed of being efficient, thoughtful, and proactive for her boss's success. It was important to her to be a secretary who made her boss successful. I will always remember her for her passion and her willingness to share it with us. She was a heroine to me too, teaching long-haired boys and bad girls how to type keys on a typewriter.

But I still felt alone. No creative outlets existed. I didn't know how to bond with the other girls. And I was pregnant for the first time. I had been so careless about it; I was surprised it hadn't happened sooner. I was deeply disappointed with myself because I was so undisciplined.

I saved money and asked a roommate to drive me to Syracuse so I could get an abortion. It was a gray February day. *Roe vs. Wade* had gone into effect three years prior. It was still socially taboo, but I was too young and too alone to care about what others thought. In the waiting room, I could see all the women lined up: young, not speaking, reading magazines as if they were interested. I wondered what they were there for – maybe a stomach-ache, cold, a sore throat. I didn't realize we are all there for the same thing.

The doctor was a man. A nurse was present. All she said was, "take your clothes off and put this on." And then, "The doctor would like to talk to you in his office, so get dressed."

In the doctor's office, I sat down across from his desk. In a soft voice, he asked, "How will you take care of yourself from now on?"

"I'll be more careful," I replied.

He stood. I remember his face even today. I remember his sadness mixed with hope for me. "I hope I don't see you here again". Then he opened his arms and embraced me (nothing inappropriate). His hug was as warm as the golden sunshine on an open field.

His hug nurtured me. I tried to do better and live right. I made a few steps in the right direction.

I graduated from this school under one condition: promising I would never, ever come back. My grades were failing, at a D+ average. The headmaster gave me a C+ so I could graduate. We shook hands on our agreement, and I got my high school diploma. I haven't been back since.

Back in Waverly, I was not experienced in conversation, and I really didn't care about what other people wanted or needed. I was energetic and creative with no outlet. I dated boys I might have been willing to introduce to my parents. Dan and I dated for five weeks. He didn't have long hair or a drug addiction and got fair grades in school. He was a little boring but normal for the average person who found school interesting.

Again, I was careless. Danny wasn't ready at all when he found out. He refused to speak to me, see me, or answer my calls. He didn't want to be trapped. I didn't blame him.

Clinics, including Planned Parenthood, were in nearby Ithaca now. I told my parents this time. They drove me to Ithaca, and I had the abortion in the hospital where I was born. The time I was with all my children in the womb was delightful. Each talked to me very clearly. They were all very happy and left with a blessing. I went home, healed, and then moved to Ithaca where I could be away from small town life.

I do not remember much about when I became pregnant for the last time. But I did not bounce back easily from the third abortion. I grieved the loss. Maybe I'd had hormonal changes. I really do not know why I was feeling like I was. I allowed myself to ponder the idea I was committing murder.

When I sought counseling from Planned Parenthood, I was told, "A person experiencing difficulty after an abortion must have been mentally unstable previously, because an abortion does not cause a person to become mental or have emotional problems." Planned Parenthood lost all credibility with me at this point.

Were women walking away from an abortion feeling complete as if they'd just been to the spa or had a mole removed while getting their hair done? Did no one experience hormonal changes after aborting their fetus? I knew I wasn't crazy. Maybe only by being procedural and cold could the clinic continue giving women their "choice."

The children who came to be with me – albeit only partly through a term – were spared the suffering of having a body in this harsh world. I know they enjoyed the moments in my warm and loving womb before we agreed it was time. They did not want to be, I felt, born into this mess.

No one can come between my children and me by saying I killed them. They knew, and God knew, what would happen. My children experienced gravity, but without being pulled down into it, like me.

When I drive past the Planned Parenthood clinic, the protesters outside hold signs of opposition to choices women make. In the minds of those protesters, they are doing their best to hold space for the unborn. But those children are not there to be born. And those women are not here to be mothers carrying to term. The women are without support from their partners who helped create the growing life inside. While Planned Parenthood will provide a choice to abort, they do not recognize the reality of needing help in grieving the loss afterwards or the hormonal changes that occur after the procedure.

I have surprised myself in things I have chosen to do and not to do in my life. What I know is that I can never know for sure who I will be and what I will decide until I have walked into the experience and had the opportunity to live it. I once judged people as wrong for some of the very things I have done. Only by being in a situation can I walk in another's shoes and understand them without judgment.

I was born because my mother got pregnant at a time when she needed support raising her children. She didn't want to be pregnant, yet she had no choice but to give birth. She gave me life in a body, though she was physically drained from it for much of her life.

I said "no" for my mother because I had a choice. I said "no" for myself because I wanted my children to have a good life.

My name is Jean. It means "God's Gracious Gift."

Appendix B: ET Residents in the "Wild"

The following pages include newsletters of the Evangelize Today Resident-Scholar-Evangelists. Each one is making discoveries in the wild, learning the way of the confessor.

Hearing the Pulse of My Parish

Harris Bond is a resident with Evangelize Today and a church planter in Monroe, Louisiana. During the COVID-19 Pandemic, Harris suffered a surprising heart attack. Here he offers his reflections on breathing, heart beats, and hearing the pulse of people within his parish.

Often after a morning run, I pause to feel my heartbeat. After a recent heart attack, pausing to feel my heartbeat and the air flow in my lungs energizes an invigorated mindfulness.

My heart beats! I am a creature; I am but dust. Yet my heart beats, blood flows, and air flows through me. I feel my fleeting frailty, *and yet* my heart beats alive to God who is infinite, eternal, and personal.

"The Lord God formed the man of dust from the ground, and he breathed into his nostrils the breath of life, and the man became a living creature" (Genesis 2:7).

There is a sublime dual awareness of what it means to be "a living creature." On the one hand, at each beat of my heart and breath of air, I am reminded of my creaturely dependence and my fleeting frailty.

> "All go to one place. All are from the dust, and to dust all return" (Ecclesiastes 3:30).

> "What is your life? For you are a vapor that appears for a little time and then vanishes" (James 4:14).

> *And yet,* the breath of life is granted to me. The beats of my heart are given to me. The air in my lungs gives life. God breathes the breath of life into me and desires me to be!

> Now, at any given moment, the noise of my plans, pains, dreams, sins, failures, and anxieties floods my soul. *And yet* God sees me and breathes upon me and is *pleased* for me to breathe. In the breathing of my lungs and the beating of my heart, all the noisy accusations and distractions of the world and my soul hush as God breathes within me. I sense His pleasure in how He created me and where He has placed me. I bear His image and live in His goodness.

> The Holy Spirit breathes new life and energy into my heart. I know Jesus and His saving power floods into my being. The same Creator, who shined light in the beginning and breathed life into me, has also shown in my heart the light of His glory in the face of Jesus Christ.

Jesus became human with a beating heart in my place and for the world. With His lungs He breathed the same air that we do. He entered the same noise and temptations of the world, sinful flesh, and the devil himself. He spoke life and healing. He hushed the demonic and natural storms with the breath of His voice. And on the Cross, His beating heart, though close to failing, faced down the ultimate sclerotic blockage of my sin. *"Then Jesus called out in a loud voice and said 'Father, into your hands I commit my spirit!' And he breathed his last"* (Luke 23:46). This King of the cosmos breathed His last, so I may breathe new life in Him, who has become a "life-giving spirit" (1 Cor 15:46).

Underneath all my neighbors' traumas and treasures deep inside, their hearts beat! Feeling my own heart beating now changes the way I approach my neighbors. My youngest child's emotional bandwidth overwhelms my own. Amidst the noise in her heart and mine, I can slow down with her and be for her. A new friend navigates traumatic childhood past, depression and anxiety, and financial instability. Yet I can pause amidst the noise in her soul and know God desires this friend to live and breathe and have her being. I can engage her with compassion and truth.

Each beat of my heart is to be for Him and for others an instrument of loving cultivation. This starts with my family and reverberates outward to my parish. *Hearing my own pulse readies me to hear the pulse of my parish.*

My own breath and heartbeat teach me the need for rest and Sabbath without guilt. *And yet* my heart beats for an eternal glory to be revealed.

God preserved me from likely death and sent me back to serve others with the Gospel "as a dying man to dying men" (to use the phrase from Richard Baxter's 1656 book, *The Reformed Pastor)*. My heart beats to be spent on others. This is my daily pursuit, to find my way into Gospel love with others.

"Oh LORD, you have brought up my soul from Sheol; you restored me to life from among those who go down to the pit ... You have turned for me my mourning into dancing ... and clothed me with gladness, that my glory may sing your praise and not be silent" (Psalm 30:3, 11-12).

The Voices In My Head **

You're not doing enough. You're an illegitimate church planter. One of the voices I hear in my head tells me, "You're not doing enough." More specifically, "You're an illegitimate church planter if you haven't already gathered people and are meeting regularly."

I acknowledge that the bi-vocational missionary approach I'm following in planting a church is not as familiar to many as is the standard approach of recruiting as many Christians as possible and starting a meeting. And so, I get this question frequently: "So, where are you meeting?" My answer to them is "Let me tell you *who* I'm meeting." I answer that way because I really believe I am called to this approach. Nonetheless, the voice in my head says, "What you're doing is not legitimate unless you're meeting."

And so, I struggle. I hate it.

But here's what I believe.

I am being true to God's calling when I am out meeting people (non-Christians) that are not inclined ever to come to a meeting,

Sunday or otherwise. I do want to meet with other Christians, but I want to meet with them to celebrate and to hear about people they are meeting, and to fervently pray for them to come to faith in Jesus. To search Scripture together and be encouraged to press on. I look forward to meeting; celebrating and encouraging each other; spurring one another on toward love and good deeds out in the wild (Heb. 10:24-25). I look forward to planning creatively when, where, and how to include the new friends we are meeting. I can't wait for regular Sunday worship – it will be amazing. That's the truth with which I want to drown out the voice in my head that says I'm not doing enough or I'm illegitimate.

But right now, more often than not, I still hear it loud and clear. Ugh!

**Although not actual voices, they are real to me and the source of ongoing internal struggle. No need to alert Presbytery... yet!

Bill Nash, Newsletter

Before

My Experience in the Wild:
Build a Parish, Build a Church

Have you ever said, "How did I miss this?" It may have been a new-to-you ice cream flavor or sautéed Brussel sprouts instead of the boiled nastiness you ate a bite of and vowed you wouldn't touch again.

God gives us these "Aha" moments of illumination about simple things but also profound things, right? He does if we slowdown in order to see them. A hurried life cannot see past the immediate and the surface.

A mentor of mine has helped me to look for what we have missed around us in people: the image of God behind layers of masks, lies, hurt, and walls. In other words, we are often looking only for what we want to see in people and gravitate toward them, the more they look like me or what I want to see in them.

I never thought about working with women and girls dealing with an unplanned pregnancy. It wasn't on my radar, as I only was looking where I was comfortable, and this wasn't. I didn't have experience with this situation. The Lord revealed to me, however, very quickly as I advocated for these parents and the lives of their unborn children, that I myself resulted from an unplanned pregnancy.

You see, my parents may not have had a plan, but God did. My conception happened under a dark and overwhelming cloud of scientific data that convincingly was shared with my parents: "You cannot have more biological children." Yet God communicates this message time and time again to the barren woman in the Old Testament: although other people in your culture will perceive your barrenness as a curse resulting from your sins, I am showing you that I am the Life Giver. I do the miraculous and the impossible to show how I operate.

God mysteriously brought about my conception and opened my mother's womb to show her and my father that He is over all things, and His ways and thoughts are above our ways and thoughts. God's plans trumped anything else. We forget that God is in the business of LIFE. In the Church, we limit God only to working in the ways we think He should work and get frustrated when He doesn't work this way.

We need to realize that God is working sovereignly to ordain not only the ends but has also the means to get to those ends. How does this help us? It keeps us from the impersonal and passionless declarations of many Muslims who say, "It is God's will" or "as God wills". God wants us to cherish not only the person's final coming to faith but also the person's process *before* they come to faith.

At the pregnancy center, we work with the parents to cultivate a sense of attachment and responsibility to their child where there is nurturing, instruction, encouragement, and sometimes confrontation *before the child is born*. Why? We want to see them continue in these patterns as there is a connection with prenatal development and how a child will handle things as a newborn.

Image-bearers who are treated as image-bearers, who treat themselves as image-bearers will also treat their children as image-bearers. How cool is it to not focus on "getting someone saved" but rather valuing God for the process? Let me tell you, it is really cool. What makes it so cool as it doesn't involve this dreaded sense of duty but rather involves a sense of delight and hope that God will work out His plan on His timetable.

This is a real-time trust of God as it is faithful to do our part but also rests on Him to do His part in His timing.

There is a peace that is so sweet for the believer who grasps this. Also, there is a greater evangelistic zeal as it doesn't seem like this grand and elaborate scheme to evangelize the world but rather is a "one person at a time" perspective. We can only do what we can do. Are we really trusting God to do what only He can do?

Dieter Paulson

My Experience in the Wild

The Birth line and the Pregnancy Center Parish

I am working on something called the birth line. A child is conceived and is alive, but it is still in a developmental process for nine months. When it is time to come into the world, the child experiences what we call birth. Strange as it sounds, we are all nine months older than we celebrate!

If we consider the spiritual journey of people, we speak of regeneration by the Spirit where they have been brought to spiritual life. Then there is conversion, where a commitment is made to follow Christ. Many Christians experience a period between regeneration and conversion that is a process of development. There are some who could say regeneration and conversion happened simultaneously. But what if God, in His infinite wisdom, is showing us, in the physical birth line of human beings, an analogy to the spiritual birth line of His people? This would have huge implications for evangelism and discipleship. We don't know when the Spirit regenerates people. Nonetheless we have a part in sowing Gospel seeds, such that we see discipleship in every interaction with image-bearers of God, who likely have amnesia about being made in the image of God.

What am I discovering in my parish around this birth line?

When a mother hears the heartbeat of her unborn child, something happens inside of her that moves her to compassion toward her child even when she has had abortion on her mind. There is a realization of who she is and who the child is, that they share something profound in common. I will call this an "image of God realization." Life sees life. Life counts life. Life bonds with life.

The fog of the image of God amnesia about oneself and the child is lifted. Deception gives way to reception. A bond is formed. Something sacred has occurred in the profane world of an unwanted pregnancy from unwed parents.

Our "Five-Question Interviews" and tattoo interviews are like an ultrasound. They are "evangelistic sonograms" that seek to find out whether there is life within or not. Mere telling an abortion-vulnerable or abortion-minded woman about the truths of God's creation and redemption, and the facts of the process and aftermath of abortion, will often shut them down and send them packing. So it is with our sharing the Gospel first with those we meet. A sonogram for the pregnant mother or couple affords treatment with dignity and care, before she (perhaps with her partner) hears what is true and what to do. It also reveals something is alive and real inside. The "evangelistic sonogram" helps them to look within, helping people see what is or isn't inside of them, maybe even seeing what is lacking in their heart, thoughts, or desires.

Both the evangelistic sonographer and the one receiving the sonogram are essential: you need both for the looking within, to happen.

Together, the sonogram and its evangelistic sequel make something happen not only in the person receiving them but also in the person doing the evangelistic sonogram. We both witness life and celebrate it.

A final thought: Is God not only the Creator but also the Perfect Sonographer?

My Experience in the Wild: The Pregnancy Center

Parish Gets Real

I know I have talked about the birth line and the life we witness at the pregnancy center. There have been some joy-filled discoveries along the way. But there have also been some very difficult discoveries as well.

One of our clients, who was expecting twins, learned that the twin girls were no longer alive. Even worse, she would have to deliver them stillborn. She did this by herself. She let me know, after her experience, that she experienced the presence of God as she held her twin girls in her hand. She showed me a picture of her two girls dressed up. My heart nearly stopped. These two girls looked very much alive yet sleeping. I just couldn't wrap my head around this moment. Even more, I don't know how she could ever wrap her head around this moment either.

A month later, she called the center and let us know that she took way too much prescription medication, intending to kill herself. We talked about some hard and painful experiences that preceded her attempt. Unfortunately, she went home and took more medication intending to finish taking her life. Thankfully, after failing again she reached out to us and we called the office of the Sheriff, who went out and took her to the hospital to get checked out. The next day we helped her get into a psych unit at a neighboring town's hospital. She learned in her time there how she was bottling up all her pain and grief. She learned that she tried to kill herself a month to the day from delivering her stillborn twin daughters. The story doesn't end there. She recently learned she is pregnant with triplets. This hasn't been easy for her. She still is profoundly grieving her loss. God has shown her that, had she been successful in killing herself in June, she would have not only killed herself but also would have prevented her three new babies! She has a unique sense that God did not want her to be successful. She still is struggling to see this pregnancy as a blessing. It is always hard for someone grieving to allow him- or herself to feel some joy or happiness without feeling guilty.

What have I learned in this episode? There are times we lament and grieve and wrestle. Grief is real. Not being able to see past the grief to see what God is doing is real.

The veil while grieving is such that you can't see past it…it takes time for your focus to be adjust and to see more clearly what God has for you.

Does the story have a happy ending? It hasn't ended so I can't say that. The story continues. My client continues to grieve; my staff, volunteers, and I also ache. The hope is there for joy to come in the morning, but weeping does last for a night. God has a purpose for our tears and our pain. It just may not be evident to us right away what the purpose is. However, it is important to hold fast to God and know that He often purposes for us to experience grief, share one another's burden, and simply walk alongside one another.

Greetings from Spartanburg

First, thank you for praying for my evangelism residency. Sorry to be giving you just an update, but I hope that this letter will give you a window into some of what the residency involves and maybe even encourage you to ask questions in the wild!

One of the goals of my residency is to interview fifty people over the coming year and ask them five questions:

1. Where do you believe the world came from?

2. What do you believe about God?

3. What do you believe about Jesus?

4. What do you believe about life after death?

5. If you could ask God one question, what would you ask him?

And yes, I actually have to find people to interview. I decided to start with someone that I already knew from the gym. We'll just refer to him as E.G. I've known E.G. for several years, and we've occasionally talked about spiritual matters, so I told him I was doing a religious residency and needed to ask people five questions about religion, and that my job was strictly to listen. (A big thrust of the residency is to try to shift from listening to reply to listening to understand). I told E.G. that he would be my first interview subject or guinea pig and that I had no idea what I was doing. Thankfully, he agreed and then we talked for about an hour. His answers were about what I expected: a hodgepodge of Christian and various other religious ideas. When we got to the last answer, he paused and thought about it a second; and then he said, "I'm not sure I'd feel worthy to ask God anything! Plus, wouldn't just being in his presence answer a lot of questions?" When I saw E.G. the next week, he said, "I'm still thinking about that last question, but I think I'm sticking with my answer." He had also told a friend about our interview and shared the last question with him as well.

My second interview was with a police officer; I volunteer as a chaplain for the department. One morning when I was praying at roll call, I volunteered to buy officers a lunch or a beer if they would help me with my religious residency by answering five questions. One officer, who had worked all night and was about to get off for the day said, "Hell yeah, I'll take you up on that!" Not exactly what I was expecting. Due to his schedule, we skipped the early morning beer and talked for about 15 minutes before he left. He gave standard Christian answers to the first four questions. But when I got to the fifth question, he stopped, thought a minute, and said, "Did I measure up?"

Please pray for these two men. Pray for me as well. The recent weeks I have been busy with my everyday pastoral work and haven't been able to work on the residency as much as I would like. Pray that I would be able to carve out the space in my schedule to get out into the wild, that I would be willing to get out of my comfort zone, and that Jesus would lead me to people to interview.

Grace and Peace, Justin Kendrick, November 13, 2019

What am I discovering?

Here's one thing I was not expecting: for people to find out I am a pastor and then confess their troubles to me as if I were Roman Catholic priest in a confessional booth.

I wasn't expecting the load to be as heavy as it is. I have an innate ability to recognize pain, to enter it, and then absorb it. My coach calls it the genius in my wound. It's a blessing and a curse. I have a compelling desire to move towards the pain, but a fleshly reaction against it because of what it costs. Lord, can I just go be a banker or a Home Depot clerk?

Demi Lovato sang a new song ("Anyone") at the 2020 Grammy awards:

A hundred million stories
And a hundred million songs

I feel stupid when I sing
Nobody's listening to me
Nobody's listening

Anyone, please send me anyone
Lord, is there anyone?
I need someone, oh
Anyone, please send me anyone…

The cry of so many people is for someone to listen. And so evangelism begins with a willingness to become emotionally engaged enough with someone to enter into their story simply in order to listen, acknowledge, and identify with their bleeding. This is what Jesus has done for us. And this is what He calls us to do for others. Do we have an answer for their cries for relief from the pain? Yes, the answer is Jesus. And if we prayerfully wait for it, those whom we hear will be open to hear what we have to say.

Take Ramey, for example (not her real name). She's a bartender. She's always busy. I noticed she has several tattoos. And recently I up and asked her if they had a story. I said, "Did you know I do tattoo research?" I gave her my card. She gave me little snippets in between taking orders for people. "This one is for my major in college, music therapy. This one is for my boyfriend who died. And I'm about to get a new one for my dad who died three months ago." Whoa! She gave me a ton of intel about her pains in a few snippets. And I get to see her every week. A one-time presentation is likely to be politely (or not) rejected. But a demonstrated willingness to hear and to hear more… well, that is evangelistic work. May the Lord bring the fruit.

Mustard Seed Evangelism

One of my main goals this year is to bring the training I have received in evangelism back into the church. I'm calling this "Mustard Seed Evangelism" because of the slow-growth nature of this style, as reflected in Jesus' parable comparing the Kingdom of God to a mustard seed, which is the smallest of seeds but eventually grows to dominate the garden (Luke 13:18-19).

One aspect of this goal is to give others the opportunity to begin with a Five-Question Interview with one of my contacts. I've now given away a few of my contacts, and it has been both thrilling and killing. Thrilling because I get to see God answer prayers to bring other AVPC'ers (AVPC: Altadena Valley Presbyterian Church) into the wild world of evangelistic interaction with non-church people. Killing because it kills my self-centered desire to build up **my** relationships with **my** non-Christian contacts. These are hard-won people I have met, gotten to know, care about, and pray for, and now I am giving them away. I think this is how it's supposed to work, right? Please pray that God continues to thrill and kill.

Mustard Seed Evangelism might just be a new paradigm for many Christians. Giving people time, respect, space, and permission to hear themselves talk and introspect about God, Jesus, salvation, and their past is a way to honor the person and trust God. This is a way to plant the mustard seed. It requires patience, waiting, and perseverance to trust that the Holy Spirit is at work.

OK, so how does this really work? What do we mean by "plant" and "seed"? We acknowledge the seed that we are offering, we don't hide or cajole or sell or bait-and-switch. We are part of a church, and we are doing research regarding topics related to Christianity. We plant by asking questions and listening well. We water by asking the person to do another five-question interview a month or so later and by texting in order to keep up (without being creepy). Baby steps. Patience, trust, prayer. No agenda other than trusting God to use us for His kingdom purposes.

Hmmm... what are you thinking? Want to give it a try?

Newsletter #13
July 15, 2020
Michael MacCaughelty
Evangelize Today Residency

The Confessor

Maybe the title for a future Liam Neeson or Denzel Washington movie? Or perhaps the biography of a prominent Catholic parish priest? Nope, it's just a role filled by simple men and women who are out in the wild and willing to listen to others. Confessor can be defined as, "a person to whom another confides personal problems." When we're willing to listen, others are eager to talk. Everybody wants to be heard but seldom do Christians take the time to listen ... we're too busy trying to figure out what to say to fix those sinners!

Obviously, this recent quarantine time has made it a struggle to get out and interact with people, but things are slowly returning to normal, and it's been interesting to see how some of my parish folks are now initiating contact with me with their hurts, stories, and even invitations to join them.

One of my parish friends called me a few days ago lamenting his feelings of depression and absence from various activities, identifying it as a spiritual pain. I was recently invited to meet a parish friend for lunch now that restaurants are beginning to open back up. Another messaged me with an invitation to join him at a nearby music venue. I've been invited to judge a karaoke contest at another local bar. (So is the shift from church pastor to bar karaoke judge a move up or down? I'll let you decide for yourself, but I tend to think it's going in the right direction.) The list could go on, but the point is that unbelievers are sharing their lives with me, inviting me in to catch a glimpse of their hearts, and demonstrating a new willingness to listen to me as I find opportunity to speak the Gospel to their situations.

Can you be a confessor? Yes, you can. You don't need to be ordained. You don't need specialized training. You don't need any unique gifting. You don't even need to become Roman Catholic. You *do* need to be available and "listen to hear" others. You *do* need to recognize your own hurts and wounds and allow God's power to use your weakness for His purposes. You *do* need to ask God to fill you with His Spirit; He will if you ask.

Thank you for your support and prayers as I continue to have a presence in the community as a confessor. Pray for these opportunities to increase exponentially in the coming weeks.

"I was only five years old."

A seventy-something-year-old widowed lady in my parish recently told me she had been sexually abused by a neighborhood kid back when she was five years old. Her unfortunate story isn't unlike many others we know. She shared this with her parents, but they didn't believe her, or if they did, they just repressed it and refused to deal with it. So, of course, the abuse continued for years, and she lived in fear, shame, and guilt. Eventually she got married and, bet you guessed it already, she suffered physical and mental abuse at the hands of her husband for years prior to his death. To this day she feels the pain of all this abuse and must relive it every time she hears of an abuse case, whether in conversation or in the media. She has become incredibly open to our conversations about Jesus, even longs for them. Indeed, she has decided to start supporting me financially. It won't be much in the world's eyes, but – according to Jesus' story about the widow putting two pennies into the offering plate – she may be one of my biggest donors (Luke 21:3).

Parish News

It was a simple question: "Would it be OK for us to have a ceremony and get married in God's eyes, but not submit a marriage certificate form to the Probate Judge?" The reason for this question was totally understandable. Once they become legally married in the state of Alabama it would more than double her health insurance premiums. (Unfortunately, there are policies and laws that discourage marriage.) As I answered, I tried to recognize their dilemma, affirm their desire to somehow honor God with a ceremony, yet also encourage them to consider the Biblical responsibility to obey the laws of the land. I wasn't trying to avoid giving them a direct answer, but I really wanted them to think through this and come to their own conclusion.

A week later this was the same person's comment. "After thinking about it, if our motive is to deceive the government just to save some money, that doesn't really honor God. So, we can't do what I was thinking about last week. Thanks for helping us think about it."

This is just a sample of what I get to see the Lord do each week in the Monday night parish group I lead. Join me in giving Him thanks for these little indications that He is definitely working in the lives of these people I care so deeply about. Please continue to pray for them!

What's New on Monday Nights?

At our most recent Monday night small group meeting at Bluegrass BBQ in Moody, one of the regular guys pulled me aside to say, "You have no idea how important this group is to my wife. She just loves it, so I'm gonna keep bringing her."

This prompted me to pause and ponder exactly why someone like her would so enjoy what we're doing. There are typically 8-12 of us. We sit and eat together, engage in some conversation, eventually I'll do a 10-minute lesson on something, we'll discuss it and often run down strange rabbit trails, I'll take prayer requests, and then I'll close in prayer. Nothing fancy, not very entertaining, no guest musicians, no fog machines, no miracle healings, etc. ... just plain fellowship, simple teaching, and brief prayer. These folks want to be loved and to express love to each other.

Lately we've been discussing some questions prompted by 1 John: Who was Jesus? Does it matter what we believe about Jesus? Does it matter what we do as Christians? What do we do with our sin? What is worldliness? What's the deal with the anti-Christ? (By the way, they loved that one!) Every week we review the Gospel and I truly believe it's taking root in their lives. Please pray for these dear folks in my parish.

A few days ago, I asked the lady cutting my hair about the

Harry Potter tattoo on her arm. She and her mom have always loved the books and movies. I suspect this tattoo is in some way a tribute to her mom. But as I asked, "What do you like about Harry Potter?" she quickly answered by noting that Harry Potter is the story of an outcast who finds family with other outcasts and who finds and pursues his unique purpose. Could it be that this lady has identified herself as an outcast, either by being labeled as such or by her own feelings of inadequacy? Though I couldn't follow up much at that time (I just don't have enough hair for a lengthy conversation), hopefully I'll be able to next time.

Under the Shade Tree

by Randy Saye

A lot has happened since my last newsletter: Covid, the death of George Floyd, protests, and riots. Meanwhile, I was supposed to continue working on my Evangelize Today Residency. There I was, standing at the intersection of all these experiences. Let me tell you a story.

Since our church wasn't holding on-site worship services and our deacon couldn't check his mailbox at the church, I began delivering his mail to his place of business every week after stopping at the post office. Then the George Floyd incident happened; followed by all the societal unrest. I was nagged by multiple questions: "What am I supposed to do? What can I do? Do I join the protests and risk being lumped in with an activist agenda I don't endorse? Do I do nothing and risk not applying the tenets of the Gospel to all areas of life?"

One day, while out delivering the mail and weighed down in contemplation, I cross the railroad tracks that divide this small southern town. I look over to my left and see a group of black folks sitting under a shade tree next to a simple house. *I understand that using the term African-American is now offensive to many.* Then I have a thought, "I'm going to pull into that driveway and have a conversation."

After delivering the mail, I drive back to house. I pull into the dirt driveway and hop out of my vehicle. The onlookers are wide-eyed and I'm laughing on the inside. They must be thinking, "What in the world is this white man up to?" I introduce myself by saying, "Hey, I'm Randy. Can I ask you guys a question?" They are cautious but accommodating. I continue, "I'm a preacher in town and it's obvious that our society is in a mess right now with the George Floyd incident, the protests, and the riots. What do folks like you want this white preacher to know?"

The answers they gave were varied. "People are just people, and we need to learn to get along." "Tell the cops to stop killing us." "Pray for us." "Give me some food." If you remember, one of the main objectives of my residency program is to learn how to listen. So, listen I did. No judgment. No counter-arguments. No presentation. I listened and we talked. I hung out and we joked with each other. Was something bigger than a one-time survey afoot?

As I spoke with my coach, Al Dayhoff, he suggested I return to the shade tree with a chair. One thing he teaches his residents is that they need to be "in the wild" – engaging with the world outside the walls of the church. He also talks a lot about having a "parish mentality." He encourages us to shepherd our flock in the brick-and-mortar church, but also to also find a flock on the outside. I took his advice and went back to the shade tree.

My new friends call me "Rev." They tell me they got my back when I'm there. *Should I be worried!?* I've brought peanuts, chicken, and pork rinds to the shade tree. They have names like Money, Rock, and Marco. They're comfortable enough to be themselves. And I've seen and heard some very colorful things under that shade tree!

What do I do when I'm there? I mostly listen. Some people call it the ministry of presence. Al likes to say that black folks are a "be with you people." What does this have to do with evangelism? If they are a "be with you people" and I'm making a point to be with them, then they are becoming my people and I am becoming one of them. It reminds me of the Scripture, "I am my beloved's and he is mine" (Song of Songs 6:3).

I think I may have found my congregation, my flock outside of the brick and mortar. Pray that God would expand His kingdom, and my heart, in this new endeavor.

:

What is Tattoo Storyhunters Trussville?

To put it very simply, I think Tattoo Storyhunters is mine and my wife's parish. When I began working with Evangelize Today in the residency I had somewhat of a fascination with tattoos, but I had no idea how to approach someone to ask them about their ink. I think I understood intuitively that there was  something of depth going on with tattoos but I had no idea what it was or how to find out. When I began working with Evangelize Today as a resident, Al Dayhoff had me do that strange and awkward thing: go up to someone and just ask them! I fumbled my way through the first several, but the people I asked were very kind and patient with me. After a few of these attempts at asking and listening I found that people actually wanted to talk. One of the first ones I thought to document with a photo belongs to a young lady has two children represented by the birds on the branch and three children who were miscarried represented by the birds flying away. This story hit me. I realized that there are indeed stories under these tattoos. I tried a few more interviews out in public, and then the Coronavirus quarantine hit, and people couldn't go out in public places as easily. I so wanted to keep going with this tattoo project but didn't have a clue how to keep it going.

 Earlier in the year my wife had gotten a small tattoo on her left wrist. She saw how much I was beginning to enjoy this tattoo research and wanted to help me. So, she posted a picture of her tattoo on our city's message group on Facebook, asking for help for her husband who was researching tattoos and looking for people to interview. We thought we might get 10-15 people willing to be interviewed. Twelve hours later there were over 300 comments with people willing to do an interview! Wow, this is great, we said. Wow, how do we do this, we said! We made a list and started working our way through it. I would meet with the guys and my wife would meet with the ladies. Sometimes we would do the interviews together.

Over time I noticed something new in the interviews. Previously, when I was just asking people in passing as I was out and about, I was getting the 30- second answer to their tattoo story. When we setup an appointed time to sit down with the people on our list, I found that we were getting the hour-long version of the story. We were completely blown away by how many people were inviting us into the deeper parts of their stories. What was going on? I learned to start asking the question, "How often have you shared all this?" Or "Have you processed all this with anyone else?" Almost always the answers were not

at all and no. Why did they open up to me and my wife? We would tell them up front that I am a pastor in the area who is learning how to listen. Over time an idea developed in our minds. We had met many people who had shared the secrets of their soul with us. We wanted to figure out what it looked like to continue to have them in our lives. Would they want us to keep in touch with them? What did that look like? Also, we wanted these folks to meet each other. We begin to envision a community forming among our tattooed friends. So, we proposed the idea of a tattoo storytellers night at the local brewery. We began sharing this idea and most people we interviewed liked the idea. One couple we interviewed happened to have some incredible musical abilities, so we asked them to provide music. They were on board. We asked a few of our previously interviewed friends to be willing to be interviewed

by us on the night. Not only were they willing, but they were excited and even felt honored that we would ask them! The night finally came, and we wondered whether no one would come and this thing would flop. We were wrong! They came, they shared, and we enjoyed great music.

It actually happened! We had a great time, and now some of our interviewees want to help us with some interviews. Some love what we are doing and want to be a part of it. This is bigger than just my wife and me. Tattoo Storyhunters Trussville now belongs to those we have interviewed and love what this is. We plan to have future gatherings of various kinds. A friend made this logo for us! This is our parish. They are ours and we are theirs.

How is this different from therapeutic deism?

This is a question that I have been asked to consider as I have ventured into the wild through the window of tattoos. It has happened numerous times now...someone that I am interviewing will say "Oh my tattoo doesn't really have any deep meaning..." but before the interview is over they are weeping over something they either didn't know was there or hadn't spoken out loud with anyone else. They might even say, "Wow! I don't know where that came from," or "It's weird to hear myself say all this. I haven't told anyone all this." Sometimes they will even say, "That was like therapy!" So there it is. Is this just like therapy? What's different about this from just going to a therapist? For one, I am not a therapist! I am a pastor. They know that going into these interviews. Because they know that about me upfront, these conversations almost always go into a spiritual direction. They speak about what they believe about God, or religion, and they are the ones who often take them there. They will often tell me they are not Christians in these conversations. If I get the chance to talk with them again, I will often ask them what it was like to be interviewed by a pastor about their tattoos. Some say that it was nice to get to talk about what they believe without judgment. I will also ask them how it is that I, a pastor, and they (non-Christians) are able to have conversations about spiritual things together now.

They will say something like, "Well, it's because you actually wanted to listen to me and understand me." The relationship was founded on trust and being open. Some come to me wanting to talk about spiritual things. Some come asking for prayer. The point is they see me not as their therapist, but as a spiritual guide.

However, I think the larger point in this discussion isn't so much that I have the answer to this question, but rather I am exploring, learning, and discovering through field work. My mentor Al Dayhoff refers to an "echo chamber." This term represents conversations and constructs that we create within the church about those outside the church, but without having gone outside the church to do the field work. We think inside the echo chamber. We talk inside the echo chamber, and then we re-think inside the echo chamber as we formulate constructs that align with our views. I am discovering just how many of these constructs are internal to me and are being undone through field work. I am finding that researching my way out of the echo chamber generates discoveries that helps me learn what is going on "out there" in the non-Christian world. What I discover often doesn't fit into my constructs, nor do the people I listen to want to be fitted into my constructs. I don't have a neatly wrapped up answer to this question, but I have learned that this question is often deconstructed when the person goes out and does field work. Therapeutic deism lacks power. When you witness the Image of God in the non-Christian speaking, and you feel the Spirit of God in you hearing and engaging with them, I think you begin to see the power of Christ at work in ways that breakdown our constructs.

When do you present the gospel?

Perhaps this is one of the most common questions that comes out as I talk about tattoo interviews. What do tattoo interviews have to do with evangelism? The question under the question is, what does listening have to do with evangelism? This question comes up perhaps most often in my own mind because I know everyone else in the church is wondering the same thing. I have constructs in me that say things such as, "It's not evangelism until you make a gospel presentation." Tattoo interviews are undoing this construct in me. What does it mean to present the gospel? Is it a packaged presentation? Too often I found in myself the feeling of needing to flip a switch, or to bring a pre-packaged presentation into the conversation, for me to feel that I was doing evangelism. Doing so felt awkward, arbitrary, and disingenuous. It felt to me that I either needed to leave Jesus out of the conversation or to convince the person to surrender to him all at once. Perhaps you can identify with that tension. In both cases I was trying to control the conversation. The Image of God in the non-Christian can sense that in us. When I began interviewing people with tattoos, I convinced myself that I was a researcher. What do researchers do? They ask questions and listen. They observe and discover. When I allowed myself to do that, I discovered that, rather than trying to present to the person, I was able to *be present* with the person I was with. When I try to control the conversation or look for a hole to slip the presentation into, I was not really connecting with the person. More importantly, I was not able to sense the leading of the Spirit of Christ in me. So perhaps the question, "When do you present the gospel?" can shift to, "When does the Spirit of Christ present the Gospel to the Image of God in the non-Christian?"

When I relinquish control of the conversation, I relinquish control to Christ. When I allow the persons to whom I am listening to know that I am taking a real interest in them and their stories, I am allowing them to experience the pursuit of God. What is God's first engagement with mankind after the first sin? Interestingly, He asks a question: Where are you? God already knew where they were, of course. So why did He ask a question? Why didn't He tell them what they did and make a presentation? Perhaps it was to give our first parents the space to say out loud, "I'm hiding...I feel exposed...I am afraid." God leaned into the fallen world with a "listening-to-hear" question. Perhaps that is the first Gospel presentation.

When I listen, hear, and hold the story of another person, trust is built. When trust is built, I find that they will listen to me. I find that we can have longer-term conversations of who God is. We can talk about the person of Jesus, and how He differs from the bad church experiences that the person may have had in the past. Listening, hearing, and holding make up the first presentation of the gospel – because listening, hearing and holding are a loving pursuit of a bearer of the Image of God.

Are tattoos an opportunity for the confessors of our age to be called out?

What is going on in a tattoo? Perhaps you can laugh with me as I, a person without tattoos, try to answer that question. I will begin with Al Dayhoff's words, "The Image of God in the non-Christian has gotten so desperate to be heard that it's writing on its wrapper in permanent ink." Are we listening? Enter the next question: what is a confessor? The Bible tells us that we ought to confess to one another that we may be healed (James 5:16). In the church we ought to be doing this for each other. If you have had the experience of confessing something personal and deep within you that you haven't shared with anyone else, you understand the "healing" that can take place. You know the feeling of a weight being lifted off you. Often there are particular people to whom others are drawn or feel safe confessing something to. This person could be identified as a confessor.

In Roman Catholic churches there are confessional booths in the back of the sanctuary. How do evangelism and confession come together? Could it be that hearing a confession is a kind of evangelism? Could it be that a tattoo is a form of confession? Often I find that the tattoo wants to speak even when the owner of the tattoo does not. The image of God, I think, is seeking out a confessor with whom to confess. The non-Christian isn't interested in going inside of a church building to find that confessor, but the desire and the need are still there.

Where do they go instead? If they are into tattoos, then it's to the tattoo artist. Perhaps one of the most amazing discoveries I have made in my tattoo interviews has come from asking the question, "How often have you shared all this?" Or, "Who else have you shared all this with?" Most of the time the answer is, "I have not shared all this to this extent with anyone else." There is a calling for confessor evangelists in our present age. We are in a time and space where dialog, listening, and conversation have been thrown out and been replaced with the megaphone of social media. Texting has replaced table conversation. The Image of God still wants to be heard. Are we listening? The confessor evangelists will listen, and tattoos might just be the gateway to realizing deep conversations.

Michael Davis, Evangelize Today Resident
Tattoo Storyhunters Trussville, Alabama

Testimonials

Al is a friend with a big ear, curious heart and concerned, loving and healing presence. He has always been very gentle in his way of discovering the person behind the mask. *Jean*

Whenever I would see Pastor Al Dayhoff enter JV's Restaurant, the "seat of his parish," it would often take him 30-45 minutes to reach my table, as people would light up when they see him, and pull him close to share or confess their deepest hopes, fears and thoughts with him. The ice in the soft drink that I would order for him, when he walked in, was always melted." *Jim*

Al was more than a confessor – he was the secret keeper for all of us at Sully's and later JV's. Always someone who would listen without judgment, counsel without lecturing, and empathize with understanding. I miss our chats immensely. *Dawn*

"Hello Al! Nice to see you! Guess what happened to me the other day? Can you believe it? What should I do? Be quiet, don't say anything!" Heard by a regular at the bar to a bar owner almost every day! And yes, Pastor Al comes with the bar – he holds Blue Church on Sundays and even does funerals in our bar. *Lorraine Campbell, owner of JV's Restaurant, Falls Church, VA*

Pastor Al really listened to me when I told him about my work helping Yezidis and Christians killed in the Middle East by ISIS. His listening to me helped me find some peace in the horrible stories of atrocities I've heard. *Susan*

Al cares for my heart and calls me to the cross and out into the Wild at the same time, where I find healing and God's pleasure. *Gary Purdy*

Confessing is risky. Usually, it brings fear and shame. But with Al, confessing makes me feel loved. Confessing with most people makes me feel shame. Confessing with Al makes me feel loved. Confessing with most makes me feel controlled. Confessing with Al sets me free. Being vulnerable can bring fear and shame. But with Al, I eagerly seek him out to share my darkest moments. He doesn't make me feel shame; he makes me feel loved. *Name Withheld*

Al has not only been a Confessor to me; he has taught me to become a Confessor for others. In the shame-filled areas of their lives, Al has taught me to see the pain, to hold it, and to bring them to a God who loves them and drives their shame away. Most importantly, in Al's presence—even when his presence is on the phone or a video chat—I have felt the love and warmth of God. *Steven Cooper, Pastor, Harbor City Church, San Diego, California*

Al is *the* person that I feel so safe with and so unconditionally loved by that, not only do I know I can tell him anything, I choose to tell him the things that I can't tell anyone else. He listens without judgement, he understands with compassion, he holds space for me to feel my feelings, and he asks questions that support my own curiosity, self-exploration, clarity, and acceptance. Al attunes to my head and my heart. And then he offers what I need in the moment, whether it's empathy, grace, wisdom, or laughter. Al is a Divine blessing in my life." *Lynette Wagner, founder of Mindfully Living LLC, contributor to Tattoos:* Telling the Secrets of the Soul, *and author of "Clear the Clutter from Your Life: Five Stepping Stones on the Path to Mindful Living and Ultimate Success."*

Al is available to listen. It's as simple as that. *Kate*

I always look forward to spending time with Al. His approach to conversations is subtle. I find that I am opening up and talking about things I hadn't planned on. And in doing so, I have allowed Al the opportunity to share thoughts that provide a different perspective, often helping me untangle a ball of yarn that I thought was untangled. *Brenda*

Hearing the secrets of the soul in a world of screaming replies. *Gary Purdy*

Wow. I have been thinking about this question for a few days. I didn't respond right away as I wanted to get my thoughts together. Al was a confessor to me. I met Al at JV's during the rocky part of my divorce. He gave me a safe place to laugh and cry. As for a quote, he said with a smile, "You aren't allowed to date for five years," just as my dad would say." *Angie*

"I'm not alone. Connecting with Al has helped me realize I'm not alone in pastoral ministry. Al and I share the same approach. As I confess to him my internal struggles with ministry and life, he listens. With Al, I know someone hears me. I'm not alone." *Bill Nash*

Al is one of those people you just feel comfortable pouring your heart out to. His presence invites openness; a few intriguing questions later, life stories flow effortlessly out, and by the end of the evening you've told some of your deepest secrets to a stranger you just met. *Briar*

Al Dayhoff is challenging the church to think differently about what Christian witness looks like in our day. My year-long residency with Al changed some of my long held Christian assumptions and provided an authentic model of engagement with others. Among other things, I learned the value of loving people simply by listening well to them. Al told me that if you can care about someone enough to just listen, it is amazing how someone will open up. Al himself exemplifies this, as I often found myself confessing things to him that I didn't intend to! Over the course of a year and many conversations with non-churched and de-churched individuals, I found his insight to be very true. The Christian world needs to learn to listen first. As Al often tells me, "the more people talk, the more they will talk themselves towards God and not away from him." *Pastor Scott Korljan, Scottsdale, Arizona church plant*

Works Cited

Irving, Washington. *Rip Van Winkle*, 1819. John Wiley & Sons, Inc. New York, NY, 1819

The Holy Bible, New International Version. Grand Rapids: Zondervan Publishing House, 1984

"Heathens" lyrics found on Suicide Squad album, 2016, Warner Chappell Music Inc. Source: LyricFind

"The Year in Review: 2020." https://www.barna.com/research/year-in-review-2020/

The Green Mile. Dir. Frank Darabont. Warner Brothers, 1999. Film.

Veronese, Keith. The Weird but True History of Sin Eaters, Posted 4/30/13 on Gizmodo, © 2020 G/O Media Inc., https://io9.gizmodo.com/the-weird-but-true-history-of-sin-eaters-479990066

Puckle, Bertram S. *Funeral Customs*. T.W. Laurie, Limited, 1926.

"Kamuysaurus." Wikipedia, Wikimedia Foundation, October 12, 2018, https://en.wikipedia.org/wiki/Kamuysaurus. Accessed September 15, 2019.

"John Vianney." Wikipedia, Wikimedia Foundation, August 3, 2004, https://en.wikipedia.org/wiki/John_Vianney. Accessed September 15, 2019.

Zucker, Steven and Harris, Beth. "The Protestant Reformation." Khan Academy, 2010. https://www.khanacademy.org/humanities/renaissance-reformation/reformation-counterreformation/beginner-guide-reforrmation/a/the-protestant-reformation.

Dayhoff, Allan. *Church in a Blues Bar.* Evangelize Today Ministries, Fairfax, VA, 2017.

Dayhoff, Allan. *Tattoos: Telling the Secrets of the Soul.* Second Edition. Evangelize Today Ministries, Fairfax, VA, 2018.

Dayhoff, Allan. *The Genius in your Wound: Life's Worst Can Reveal Your Best.* Evangelize Today Ministries, Fairfax, VA, 2019.

"Imagine" lyrics found on Imagine album, 1971, John Lennon, Yoko Ono, and Phil Spector.

"The Gates of Hell." Wikipedia, Wikimedia Foundation, July 19, 2005, https://en.wikipedia.org/wiki/The_Gates_of_Hell. Accessed September 15, 2019.

"Daredevil." Wikipedia, Wikimedia Foundation, November 3, 2004, https://en.wikipedia.org/wiki/Daredevil_(Marvel_Comics_character) . Accessed September 15, 2019.

"Hitchhiker's Guide to the Galaxy." Wikipedia, Wikimedia Foundation, November 17, 2001, https://en.wikipedia.org/wiki/The_Hitchhiker%27s_Guide_to_the_Galaxy. Accessed September 20, 2019.

"Johari Window." Wikipedia, Wikimedia Foundation, September 25, 2004, https://en.wikipedia.org/wiki/Johari_window. Accessed September 10, 2019.

"Love is a Battlefield" lyrics by Pat Benetar found on Live from Earth album, 1983, MCA Whitney Studios.

"World without Heroes" lyrics by Kiss found on The Elder album, 1981, Ace in the Hole Studios.

"Free Bird" lyrics by Lynyrd Skynyrd found on a single, 1974, Studio One.

"Hard Days' Night" lyrics by the Beatles found on Studio album, 1964, EMI, London.

"Substitute" lyrics by The Who found on a single, 1971, Olympic Studios.

"Twilight Zone" lyrics by Golden Earring found on album Cut, 1982, Polygram.

"Is there more" lyrics by Drake found on album Scorpion, 2018, Cash money.

"Creep" lyrics by Radiohead found on album Pablo Honey, 1992, Parlophone-EMI.

"St. Francis of Assisi." Wikipedia, Wikimedia Foundation, December 13, 2001, https://en.wikipedia.org/wiki/Francis_of_Assisi. Accessed September 12, 2019.

"Jacques Cousteau." Wikipedia, Wikimedia Foundation, February 25, 2002, https://en.wikipedia.org/wiki/Jacques_Cousteau. Accessed September 12, 2019.

Cousteau, Jacques-Yves and Frederic Dumas. *The Silent World. Harper and Brother Publishers*, 1953.

"Jane Goodall." Wikipedia, Wikimedia Foundation, March 22, 2002, https://en.wikipedia.org/wiki/Jane_Goodall. Accessed September 12, 2019.

"David Attenborough." Wikipedia, Wikimedia Foundation, August 31, 2002, https://en.wikipedia.org/wiki/David_Attenborough. Accessed September 18, 2019.

"Steve Irwin." Wikipedia, Wikimedia Foundation, February 1, 2003, https://en.wikipedia.org/wiki/Steve_Irwin. Accessed September 7, 2019.

"Holocene Extinction." Wikipedia, Wikimedia Foundation, November 28, 2001, https://en.wikipedia.org/wiki/Holocene_extinction. Accessed September 7, 2019.

"Fred Rogers." Wikipedia, Wikimedia Foundation, October 25, 2002, https://en.wikipedia.org/wiki/Fred_Rogers. Accessed September 4, 2019.

Tuttle, Shea. *Exactly As You Art: The Life and Faith of Mister Rogers*. W.M.B Eardmans Publishing, 2019.

Won't You Be My Neighbor? Dir. Morgan Neville. Tremolo Productions, 2018. Film.

Rogers, Fred. *Mister Rogers' Parenting Book: Helping to Understand Your Young Child*. Running Press, 2002.

"Finding Fred: Invisible to the Eye." Apple Podcasts. iHeart radio and Fatherly. https://podcasts.apple.com/us/podcast/invisible-to-the-eye/id1477279443?i=1000457214048

Saint-Exupery, Antoine de. *The Little Prince*. Mariner Books, 2000

The Lord of the Rings: Two Towers. Dir. Peter Jackson. New Line Cinema, 2002. Film.

Carroll, Lewis. Alice's Adventures in Wonderland. Macmillan, 1865.

"Myrmecology." Wikipedia, Wikimedia Foundation, September 25, 2003, https://en.wikipedia.org/wiki/Myrmecology. Accessed September 26, 2019.

"Helen Keller." Wikipedia, Wikimedia Foundation, December 7, 2001, https://en.wikipedia.org/wiki/Helen_Keller. Accessed September 23, 2019.